Surrender

and discover the abundant life

Surrender

and discover the abundant life

Louise Y Allard

Surrender and Discover the Abundant Life

Trilogy Christian Publishers A Wholly Owned Subsidiary of Trinity Broadcasting Network

2442 Michelle Drive Tustin, CA 92780

Rights Department, 2442 Michelle Drive, Tustin, CA 92780.

Trilogy Christian Publishing/TBN and colophon are trademarks of Trinity Broadcasting Network.

For information about special discounts for bulk purchases, please contact Trilogy Christian Publishing.

Trilogy Disclaimer: The views and content expressed in this book are those of the author and may not necessarily reflect the views and doctrine of Trilogy Christian Publishing or the Trinity Broadcasting Network.

Cover picture by Bonnie Ziegler, Uganda, 2012. Used with her permission.

Manufactured in the United States of America

10 9 8 7 6 5 4 3 2 1

Library of Congress Cataloging-in-Publication Data is available.

ISBN: 979-8-88738-129-9

E-ISBN: 979-8-88738-130-5

Dedication

Therese Prevost–Allard

In the Lord, 1920 to April 2022

My Life Inspiration

Acknowledgments

A journal collection that accounts for my trips to Africa forms the basis for this book. There are many people whom God has placed in my life to enable me to go to Africa, and more frequently to Uganda, for the last twenty years. Some inspire a life of service, some model it, and some remain at home and provide an anchor for my life, always welcoming me back with excitement and interest in the work. There are board members and advisors who keep me accountable and focused, both here and in Uganda, and there are supporters and donors. There is someone who encouraged me to write this book; there are those who reviewed it and gave their best advice. There is God who called and enabled me to live it. Here are my helpers:

- Jesus Christ, who called and redeemed me, "Christ the power of God and the wisdom of God" (1 Corinthians 1:24, NIV).

- My mom, Therese Prevost-Allard, who was a woman of great strength, devotion, and desire to follow the path of righteousness at any cost.

- Eithne Keegan, who inspired me to serve abroad, who modeled it, and who lived it with me on several occasions, a woman of God and deep faith, always pursuing her calling despite numerous health challenges.

- The anchors: my son, Steven, my daughter, Caroline, and my aunt, Micheline, who came to Uganda with me in 2009; my friends Kathy, Joy, Alexis, Golie, Brigitte, Sharon, and my brothers and sisters.

- Board members of Alliance for Life International (ALI) in the US: Dennis Rasmussen, JD; Dr. Sergio Stone, MD, ob-gyn; Stephen Meyer, PhD in psychology; our advisors: James Wale, financial expert, and Bruce Sonnenberg, founder/director of He Intends

Victory, Eithne Keegan, CEO of Hospital Christian Fellowship and my mentor.

- Board members of ALI-Uganda (ALI-UG): Cyprian Biribonwa, Dr. Sandra Nabachwa, MD, Dennis Rasmussen, JD.

- Board members of St. Raphael Healing and Wellness Center: chair Chancellor Dominic Ndugwa, Cleophus Mugenyi, PhD, Cyprian Biribonwa, business owner, Florence Butegwa, JD, Father Francis-Xavier Magezi, Godfrey Segujja, project coordinator, chair, finance/fundraising John Byabasaija, technical chair Joseph Kitone.

- A dedicated group of supporters and donors, including Father Sy Nguyen, Deacon Denis Zaun, and their congregation at St. Martin de Porres Church in Yorba Linda, California.

- Bob Goff, JD, author, and a Ugandan honorific recipient, who encouraged me to write this book.

- Deborah Marchica, Eithne Keegan, and Carol Krejci, friends and book editors.

I am very grateful to all who have played an extraordinary role in my life and are sharing the journey with me.

Table of Contents

Foreword

We work to encourage Christians in healthcare by mentoring, discipling, and providing tools to equip them for their spiritual walk at the bedside or wherever they touch people's lives.

I have walked alongside Louise as a friend and mentor for the past twenty years. We met at Saddleback Valley Community Church (SVCC) in 2002 while I was assembling a team of nurses for a mission trip to Congo. Little did I know that I was meeting a woman of Louise's caliber and courage and that God was calling me to be her mentor on her missionary journey!

Louise has always had a heart for children and pregnant mothers. She became certified in the Billings Ovulation Method (BOM) to help families to achieve or postpone pregnancy naturally, and she has been highly successful in teaching this program globally. She was soon to embark on a bigger adventure, the hospital project, that only God could help her achieve. It would be an impossible task for her on her own. With God, nothing is impossible!

Our second missionary journey was to Uganda and Kenya to work with those affected and infected by HIV/AIDS. I saw God planting a seed in Louise's heart. I watched how God watered and nourished it as He envisioned a pregnancy resource center, an NGO—Alliance for Life International, Uganda, and now the foundation of the St. Raphael Teaching Hospital of Western Uganda.

Louise noticed a great need for specialized doctors and nurses with advanced degrees in Uganda. She saw that they had to travel abroad at a great sacrifice to themselves, their families, and friends. Louise envisioned a teaching hospital where they could study at home and not take their knowledge elsewhere, thus leaving a void of specially trained doctors and nurses in their native country.

The plans are in place; the next step is to begin the construction of the St. Raphael Hospital, starting with the children's facilities. The verse that comes to mind is: "Trust in the LORD with all your heart and lean not on your own understanding; in all your ways submit to him, and he will make your paths straight" (Proverbs 3:5–6, NIV).

You will see the hoops that Louise has had to jump through and the enormous sacrifices she has encountered to build this hospital in the midst of Africa. Louise's missionary journey will inspire and encourage you. We pray that her zeal and endurance will bring this teaching hospital to fruition.

By Eithne Keegan

CEO of Healthcare Christian Fellowship, USA

MSN, RN, FCN, CNML

PART 1
THE CALL TO SERVE

Chapter 1. Who Is God Calling?

Your eyes saw me unformed; in your book all are written down; my days were shaped, before one came to be.

Psalm 139:16 (NABRE)

How Does One End Up in Africa?

The first and most frequent question I encounter when I share about my work in Africa is, "How did you get involved in going to Africa?" In general, people are interested in Africa, but it still represents an exotic destination, an unknown land with a reputation for tribal conflicts, strange diseases, and immense natural beauty.

As I reflect and seek to explain how one gets involved as a medical missionary, going back to Africa repeatedly for the last twenty years, it is important to realize that God is doing *the calling*. In order for you to understand how He works in one's life and accomplishes His purposes, it may help to share how God shaped me for this work and how He views each person in His realm. Here are some excerpts of Psalm 139 that express the unique perspective of God and His plans for each one of us:

> LORD, you have probed me, you know me: you know when I sit and stand; you understand my thoughts from afar. You sift through my travels and my rest; with all my ways you are familiar. [...] Behind and before you encircle me and rest your hand upon me. [...] Where can I go from your spirit? [...] If I take the wings of dawn and dwell beyond the sea, even there your hand guides me, your right hand holds me fast. [...] You formed my inmost being [...] my days were

shaped before one came to be. How precious to me are your designs, O God; how vast the sum of them!

Psalm 139:1–3, 5, 7a, 9–10, 13a, 16b–17 (NABRE)

I invite you to find out how He worked in my life. I hope you recognize His ways, His love, His guidance and provisions. You may even hear His calling.

Who Is God Calling?

I grew up in the province of Quebec, Canada. My dad was a station manager for the Canadian National Railway. My mom was trained as a schoolteacher. I was the third child in a family of seven, four girls and three boys.

Dad was a college graduate; this was not very common during the war. He was kind, articulate, and bilingual. My father loved teaching the last three younger siblings. He would have contests between them to list all the states in the US and their capitals. A dictionary was ever-present. The grandchildren were also encouraged to look up words, even before they knew how to read! He had a great sense of humor and loved plays on words. Dad loved adventure. My younger siblings remember car excursions and picnics under a bridge in the middle of winter.

As in many families, there was a significant level of dysfunction. My mom did not seek outside help. Our family suffered in silence. Moreover, because no one stepped in, it got worse and worse.

Dad worked for forty years for the same organization. His faithful attendance at work gave all of us a strong message: work is essential. As a result, not one of us had difficulty with employment. We all retired after a fulfilling career.

Even though Mom never worked outside the home as a teacher, we all benefited from her expertise. Mother devoted herself tirelessly to our upbringing. When we reached teenage years, she went to work to supplement the family income. Mother was a tremendous example of tenacity and resourcefulness. Up until her recent passing at the age of 101, she remained engaged in life and a source of inspiration for me.

Interestingly, despite family conflicts, we grew up very close to one another. Church and school provided stability, and my faith in God sustained me. I was very close to my two brothers Jacques and Denis. We were only one year apart. I was involved in sports and enjoyed wrestling with them. That must have stemmed from my competitive nature.

I had a happy childhood overall. In my teen years, the dysfunction worsened. Going to nursing school at age seventeen provided a timely outlet.

It was then that I abandoned the practice of my faith. I had lost track of the rituals' meaning and felt disconnected from God. It was 1965, the beginning of very dark years for me and the culture in which I lived. I was a saint as a child but not as a young woman living without God in her life. The sexual revolution affected me.

My older sister kept to her traditional ways. Her marriage in the church survives to this day despite difficulties along the way. However, the grace that comes from the sacrament of marriage was there. Mine did not survive. We built on sand. Even though we got married in the church, I was not a believer at the time. I recall I did not accept all the words in my vows, especially those about being submissive to my husband. Our marriage lacked a solid foundation.

Getting Married

Sorry, I am getting ahead of myself. Since the age of nine, I had decided that I would marry someone from an old civilization. In Catholic school, we were often raising money for evangelism abroad. I acquired a card collection; each card had a picture of a Chinese child on it. They sold it for twenty-five cents apiece. I prayed for these children so that they would come to know the Lord. Through this practice, I believe, God gave me an international heart, although I did not grow up wanting to become a missionary.

I met my husband when I was nineteen years old. I was in nursing school at the time, studying in a large pediatric hospital in Montreal. Student nurses used to go dancing at the University of Montreal social center, a good place to meet eligible men. This tall, dark, and handsome gentleman asked me for a dance. I found out he was Egyptian Catholic, spoke Arabic, French, and English fluently, and his name was Antoine. I *loved* that name! To my delight, he came from a 5,000-year-old civilization, so he met all my requirements. It was love at first sight. We married two years later.

My Calling as a Nurse

From infancy, my younger brother Rejean required frequent hospitalizations. Around age four, he finally underwent an effective surgery. Because I was very close to him, my mom would allow me to visit him in the hospital. In those days, visiting hours were limited: two to four in the afternoon and seven to eight in the evening. I still remember Rejean standing in his crib, crying, when I would say goodbye through the windows. By the time I was eight years old, I had experienced two surgeries myself. I knew a lot about hospitals. It was then that I decided to become a pediatric nurse.

Years later, when I became a pediatric head nurse at Hoag Hospital in Newport Beach, these memories stayed with me. I was able to make some crucial changes that would help children in the healing process. I found that God was about completing what He had started. I was eight years old when my brother and I lived the trauma of separation in the hospital. I was thirty-two when God used me to make a change that would positively impact children, their families, and healthcare providers for years to come.

My Working Life as a Young Mother

When I was studying for my degree in community nursing in Canada, I was working full-time. I became exhausted with all the roles I was trying to play. We got married in 1970. Antoine and I decided that my professional career mattered and that we would accomplish our goals as partners. In theory, it sounded good, but in practice, it was very hard. I certainly would get an *A* for *trying* to be the perfect wife, the perfect student, the perfect worker, and the perfect mother. Naturally, I was not perfect at anything!

I recall a perfume commercial: the woman is cooking at the stove; she wears an elegant dress covered with a fancy apron. The voiceover says that she can earn and cook the bacon and be seductive to her husband. She can do all things well. It was the culture's idea of what it meant to be a successful woman. I felt pressure to live up to these expectations, so I worked very hard. After a challenging weekend, we decided that I would work part-time. My son, Steven, was two years old at the time. Two years later, I gave birth to our daughter, Caroline, and I fully enjoyed being a mom. I was not in school during that period either, so it was a great family time.

Going to California

My husband's family had moved from Canada to California one by one. We paid them a visit in 1976, and naturally, we liked it there. The working opportunities for us were excellent. There was great socio-political unrest in Quebec at the time, which affected us. Therefore, we decided to move. In January 1978, we established ourselves first in Chino, where Antoine's brother lived. Two years later, we moved to Mission Viejo, a new community built around a twenty-four-acre man-made lake and advertised as the California Promise!

I was very insecure in my twenties. Looking back, I believe that not having God in my life left me anxious and without guidance or wisdom to resolve my daily struggles. As a nursing student, I witnessed a doctor severely reprimanding the head nurse. The supply cart was missing essential trays that he needed to care for extremely ill children. It traumatized me. I felt that I needed to be more mature to work in pediatrics, my field of specialty.

My son's illness at age two would lead me back to my first love. Steven suffered from a grave respiratory condition that even required resuscitation. He received such excellent care that I promised myself, or maybe God, I do not recall, that I would work in pediatrics as soon as feasible.

When I started working in California, I kept my promise. A position opened up as a charge nurse. I returned to school part-time and took some healthcare-administration classes to give me increased knowledge and confidence.

My Way Back to God

It was around that time that I experienced a profound conversion. I committed my life to Christ and invited the Holy Spirit to fill me with His presence.

Our lives had all the appearance of going well. My husband and I had good management positions, and we had only been in the country for three years. We had bought a beautiful house in Mission Viejo, and it seemed as if we were living the California dream.

When I arrived in California, people would often ask me where I went to church. They were neighbors or nurses I worked with, or even strangers in the elevator. I always said that I was not going to church. Sometimes I would add that where I came from, people had stopped practicing their faith a long time ago. A deep silence would settle afterward.

In early 1981, I met Erika, my new neighbor in Mission Viejo. She asked me about my faith background. I found myself reciting some Christian beliefs: "I believe in God the Father, the Son, and the Holy Spirit"; "I believe that Jesus died for my sins"; "I believe the Ten Commandments." Erika then invited me to a Bible study at the Lutheran church she attended. I enjoyed learning about my faith in Christ, and I started attending a charismatic service at their church.

This experience eventually led us to Faith Fellowship, a nondenominational, evangelical church in Laguna Hills. We started going as a family. This young congregation was on fire for God; they displayed all the gifts of the Spirit. I began reading and studying the Word of God. I shared Christ with others and prayed for everything. Miracles followed. Here is just one to give you the flavor of what I was living. I was attending the University of California, Fullerton, on the weekends.

One Saturday, I crossed a vast boulevard with many cars going in each direction. It was probably with twelve lines of traffic and led to the university parking lot. There were tire spikes on the ground and going the wrong way. I had not noticed it was an exit, not an entrance! My husband's new car went entirely over them. Why should I take responsibility? The car was driving itself! I was expecting the worst:

tires pierced to shreds. I got out of the car and checked them. I could not see anything wrong, but then I imagined getting back to my car at the end of the day and finding my tires flat to the ground. So, I prayed earnestly.

I recounted my experience to my schoolmates. They were anxious to see what happened next. Nothing! My tires were in perfect shape. It was a great testimony.

1984

Then 1984 came, a time of testing, our worst year ever. It started with my husband losing his job in December 1983. I recall listening to the TBN Santa Ana TV station while I was decorating the Christmas tree and crying out to God. I have been a supporter ever since. I loved Paul and Jan Crouch, the founders of TBN. They became part of the family of God, along with pastors and teachers, during an intense period of my learning and getting close to God.

Financial distress came. We tried to sell the house but could not; it eventually sold for the mortgage balance. It represented a tremendous financial loss for us. However, it was a profound spiritual lesson for me. I was very materialistic at the time. I came to view the loss as part of the cure.

We looked for a house to rent in a highly competitive market. I prayed for a comparative home in South Orange County, but the rentals were terrible. Whenever there was a nice home, it was gone immediately.

I discovered that I was a daughter of the King; therefore, I would not live in a dilapidated house. I found a beautiful single-family home on the corner of Morning Star and Sweet Grass in Lake Forest. These beautiful names held profound meaning for me, a sign of God's providence. The property owner had the house freshly painted inside and put in brand-new landscaping. He loved us. By that time, things were looking up; my husband had found suitable employment.

At the beginning of 1984, we found out we were pregnant, probably due to the stress of my husband losing his job. I was distraught when I found out that he had not been paying the mortgage for months.

I wanted to divorce. My husband begged me not to. That morning, he started reading the Bible; this was unusual. He read the chapter where Jesus was selecting some of His disciples (Luke 5:1–11). He noted that they were a ragtag bunch. So, he said, "See, they were not perfect people, but God chose them anyway!" He was right, and we remained together.

It was also a time of testing my new pro-life views. After all, we became pregnant during the worst time of our marriage. However, with God's grace, we both accepted it; we even saw this as God's intervention to save our marriage. Sadly, three months later, I miscarried.

My husband and I separated in November of that year. I felt I had to shield my income to allow me to care for our children. We got back together two years later at my request. I wanted our children, who were teenagers at the time, to experience a marriage that worked. It went well for a while. He devoted himself to the children, encouraging their schooling and providing for their needs.

When I noticed that my husband suffered from compulsive behavior that jeopardized our financial security, I immediately joined a twelve-step program. In this setting, the spouses and family members who live with the affected individual find support and information. It helped me understand the disturbing habit. I realized that I was powerless to change it. It led me to focus on myself, the only person I could change with God's help. I began a period of intense self-examination. I found that I was prompt to resolve all matters regarding the children without consulting my husband. It was unbalanced and disrespectful toward him. I made repeated efforts to correct my shortcomings. Although this was an example to my husband that change was possible, he did not modify his conduct.

I set up an intervention in 1987. A professional Christian family counselor prepared me and the children. The day for the intervention finally arrived. The children and I read statements that detailed the hardships caused by the harmful behavior. He felt trapped. He had to join a twelve-step program, attend weekly counseling sessions, and stop the negative habit. If he refused, he would have to leave home and would not have visiting privileges for a time or until he sought help.

My husband agreed to the plan. He probably abstained for one to two years. Our lives improved. However, it killed the love he had for me.

When we divorced twelve years later and I asked why, he immediately cited the intervention. When our son dropped out of college after two years, my husband wanted us to stop all contact with him until he returned to school. I refused to do this, but he held to his idea and stopped communicating with our son for three years. When our daughter got pregnant, he again refused to see her for three years. He did not see our grandson until he was six years old. Later on, I read that professional interventions based on coercion do not work out in the long term. Love is a better approach.

Nineteen eighty-four was a terrible year for us, but in retrospect, God's presence, strength, and guidance were available all along. For me, the Word of God provides daily sustenance. Sometimes, I took some actions, like setting up the intervention, without ensuring it was the best thing. God did not condemn me for it. He deals with my weaknesses, like taking things into my own hands.

Pro-Life Activism

My pro-life activism started in 1983 when I saw a documentary on abortion and read a booklet entitled *When You Were Formed in Secret; Abortion in America*. I was shocked to learn that abortion was legal throughout the nine months of pregnancy and for any reason. I attended seminars and devoured writings on the subject. I have been involved in all aspects of the pro-life movement ever since, including obstructing abortion clinics as part of Operation Rescue in 1989. I felt that this represented the end of the road for me. I paid a $300 fine; a repeat offense would add a six-month jail sentence. As a mother of teenagers, I felt it was not reasonable for me to risk jail. The Lord did not require this of me.

However, I still had this huge burden to make a difference for the preborn child. I went back to school, first to complete my bachelor of science in nursing (BSN). As a follow-up, I was thinking of a law degree with a focus on bioethics. Instead, the Lord led me to Simon Greenleaf University, close to my work in Anaheim. It had become

Trinity Law School by the time I graduated with a human-rights master of arts degree in international human rights. This program enabled me to declare the rights of the preborn child. It became the subject of my thesis.

Now that I had my BSN, I became director of nursing for the home-health agency where I worked. It took me a whole year to write my thesis.

I was up to Chapter 8, the most demanding section. All my human-rights knowledge would come to bear in my defense of the right to life of the preborn child. It grew to thirty pages. I was using a word processor; I pressed the wrong key, which erased the whole chapter. I cried over it for an entire week.

I felt that my second write-up would not be as good. I poured my heart out to God and found comfort there. He reassured me that whatever He had revealed to me in the first place would come back to me. I used my notes to reconstruct the paper. It was better than the first. Later on, I realized that God allows you to go through this kind of frustration because He plans to use you for more complex things for which He is preparing you.

Human Rights

As part of my studies in human rights, I needed to attend the Institute of Human Rights in Strasbourg, France. My husband was opposed to it because of the extra expense. I prayed, and the money miraculously came when I needed it, so I went.

Someone stole my wallet on the plane. When I arrived in France, I went out for dinner and could not find my wallet when it was time to clear the bill. I was in shock for three days because of stress, heat exhaustion, and the lack of proper ventilation in my room. I had lost the means to pay for weekend travels.

Why would God allow such a thing? His Word guided me to scriptures that talked about the poor, and I found that I lacked sensitivity toward them. I lived at the university dorm with human-rights students from all over the world, most of them from Africa. Like me, they did not have the opportunity to explore other countries. Therefore, we spent lots of time together.

As a human-rights student, I asked God to use me to make a difference in grievous human-rights concerns. Soon after my arrival, I attended a reception for new students. I met Abijou, a lawyer who was involved in pressuring the king of Morocco to liberate more than 400 prisoners of conscience. Abijou was himself persecuted in his country and was looking for support. I sought the Lord because I could not see how I could help.

The next day, here was Abijou reading an Arabic newspaper. He said, "Louise, read the names of the 400 prisoners."

These people became real to me. I told Abijou that God could turn the heart of the king wherever He would wish (Proverbs 21:1). I prayed for their release after I checked with Abijou: "They're not criminals, are they?"

The following Friday, my friend the lawyer was leaving for London for a four-day trip. Abijou and other activists would write a petition to the king during that time. It was the July 14 weekend, *La Fete de la Bastille*. Indeed, I should have been going to Switzerland with my friends if only I had had money!

God kept me at the institute for a particular purpose. I prayed for Abijou and the success of his appeal.

On Monday evening, my friend arrived back at the school, in this vast lobby, and came directly to me. He hugged me and told me that the king had released most of the prisoners. Abijou said, "It is your God who did it. Thank Him so much."

What a caring and powerful God we serve!

A Miraculous Encounter

The following year, I went to China to attend the 1995 women's conference in Beijing. One of my goals was to meet up with the Billings team, who were also attending. They were there to promote the Billings Ovulation Method of natural family planning. On the first and second days of the conference, I looked for them all over. Because of rain and wind, the tents were down on the ground, and it was impossible to locate the team. I prayed earnestly.

On the third day, I took a different bus, and at the next stop, I noticed a nun as she was taking her seat; she was wearing a name tag that said, "Billings." Alleluia, she was part of the Billings delegation!

Meeting the Billings team was a turning point in my life. I met with Dr. Kevin Hume, a medical doctor who was supporting Drs. John and Evelyn Billings in their efforts to promote the method all over the world. Dr. Hume gave me a refresher on the use of the Billings method during premenopause. He was also very knowledgeable about human rights. Dr. Hume strongly encouraged me to become a Billings ovulation-method teacher. I promised him I would do it once I completed my human-rights degree.

Human Rights and the Right to Life of the Preborn Child

I attempted to publish my thesis but did not find support. However, I sent it to several pro-life, pro-family organizations. Subsequently, I had great satisfaction in observing that these organizations were using human-rights language to defend the rights of the preborn child. In addition, my thesis was available in the students' library at Trinity Law School in Santa Ana. A new generation of lawyers had access to it and acquired a human-rights perspective in defending the right to life of the preborn child.

I visited the Pontifical Academy for Life in Rome in 2001. I gave the academy's secretary a copy of the thesis declaration. I left it in safe hands.

After I graduated in 1997, I started a nonprofit human-rights organization called Alliance for Life International. The goal was to educate the public about the humanity of the preborn child and defend his or her right to life. After four years of struggling, I did not feel we were making progress. I always knew that we would find a way to live these pro-life beliefs, but I did not know how to proceed.

I had been seeking the Lord for years. When I started going to Africa,

God began to realize His greater purpose.

Our mission is to build cultures of life in which preborn children are welcome. We defend the lives of those who are most vulnerable such as the preborn child, the disabled, and the elderly. The lack of essential medical care in Uganda reflects the serious healthcare inequalities found in less developed countries. It leads us to cooperate with leaders to bring modern medical care to Uganda.

As promised, I took the Billings ovulation-method training course in 1998 and became a teacher in early 1999. Unfortunately, my marriage ended at that time. The devil will always try to stop you from accomplishing God's purposes. Things were reasonably quiet before the devastating blow. Whatever was happening was not explicit. Still, I was attempting to improve our relationship, but he would have none of it. He was indifferent.

The End of Our Marriage

In January 1999, after attending church with me, which was surprising since he had not for the preceding two years, my husband started packing a few things. I said, "Where are you going?" He said he needed to take some time to sort things out in his life. I answered, "But who is going to take care of you?" I loved my husband. That is why it hurt so much when he left.

Two days later, he announced that he wanted a divorce. When my husband came to pick up his belongings, he said, "You live your whole life as if there is a God and there is an afterlife. You are wasting your life!"

Do you remember the scripture about the unbelieving spouse? "If he wants to leave, let him go" (1 Corinthians 7:15, paraphrased). It did not come easily.

Recovering from the divorce after thirty years of marriage was heart-wrenching. God knows the pain and destruction caused by divorce, especially for the children. Thankfully, ours were young adults by that time. I kept busy with work, but I made sure I had plenty of rest. Very early on, I saw my doctor. I refused antidepressants but accepted counseling. I wanted to grieve normally, not painlessly.

A few days after the separation, I joined a divorce-support group at church. It allowed a safe space to share with people going through similar experiences and take actions that would promote healing.

When my husband left, our daughter, Caroline, was already staying with me. She was pregnant at the time. A few months later, my grandson, Gylan, was born. What a great joy! He compensated for the heartache.

I had been wearing my wedding band, but at the six-month mark, my ring broke; it was a freak accident. The Lord told me it was time to move on. My healing was not complete, but it was time to look forward. It took me five years to fully recover and accept my new identity as a single person. It was a time filled with introspection and finding God's renewed purpose for my life.

Too Much of a Good Thing

After sixteen years of pro-life involvement, from 1984 to 2000, I finally realized that I was obsessed with pro-life work. I could never do enough. Why was I feeling this incessant burden despite years of activism and studies? As if it all was on my shoulders.

You recall the scripture where Jesus says, "For my yoke is easy, and my burden is light" (Matthew 11:30, NIV). I sure was not living by it! I asked the Lord why I felt this way. He revealed that it began when I was twenty years old, fresh out of nursing school. Two of my best friends were seeking an abortion. I was living close to Montreal. They wanted my support while they would be recovering from their abortions in the big city. These requests happened during the same year. My reaction at the time was, "Are you sure you want to do this?" I do not recall trying to dissuade them.

I should have tried because, as a nurse, I had taken classes in biology. I knew this was a child in his early phase of development. At any rate, I put these experiences behind me until I became educated on the issue of abortion in 1983. After years of activism, I finally prayed that God would forgive me for my inappropriate response to the abortions. I continue to do all I can, but God delivered me from this all-consuming obsession. It may be that the Holy Spirit used my intense feelings about abortion to guide my studies and work in Uganda.

Going Back to My Roots

I continued to be involved in the Salt & Light Ministry at SVCC until 2006, capping nineteen continuous years of service in this public-affairs ministry. We sought to educate and encourage Christians to make a difference for good in our decaying culture. Once our ministry folded, I found myself free to go back to my roots and worship God in a Catholic setting.

The transition happened gradually. As a Billings teacher, I attended seminars regularly. Mass attendance was usually on the agenda.

The Billings method was born in the church and developed by two Australian physicians, also husband and wife and devout Catholics. The teaching always included a biblical exposition on human sexuality and marriage, sharing the vast knowledge from our magisterium. In 2006, I found myself crying during the entire mass at a seminar in Merced.

I came home puzzled and started praying. Someone else was praying for me at the time. Her name is Sue; she was the director of the Billings Ovulation Method Association, USA (boma-usa.org). She sent me some Christian material and encouraged me to explore my faith.

I realized that the things I was most passionate about, such as human rights and natural family planning, resulted from my Catholic upbringing. I feel complete, having experienced the practice of my Christian faith from different perspectives. I am the perfect hybrid believer!

Total Surrender

In July 1998, after I started Alliance for Life International and received news of our incorporation in California, I experienced a move of God that led me to total surrender.

There was a basket in front of me, filled with office supplies. I said, "Lord, this basket represents my life. There are all kinds of important matters in it. You are first, then my marriage, our children, my work as a nurse and for the alliance. Do You see the basket of my life? You can do whatever You want to do with it. I would like to devote myself to the work of the alliance. Lord, You have my permission to do whatever You want. I would even go to Africa!"

I had never thought about going to Africa. I was afraid of Africa. I did not like poverty, and I was terrified of strange diseases. I meant, "Lord, I would do anything as long as it is Your will."

Chapter 2. Congo First, the Safest Place on the Earth

Though an army besiege me, my heart will not fear, though war break out against me, even then I will be confident.

Psalm 27:3 (NIV)

The idea of actually going to Africa came in late 2002. SVCC was holding a mission weekend. Pastor Rick Warren encouraged us to go worldwide on short-term mission trips to spread the gospel of peace. It meant contributing our experiences and skills, sharing our faith in the mission field, and developing Christian leaders. A very insistent parishioner signed me up for an information night about a trip to Congo in April 2003.

Dr. Sergio welcomed me and talked to me at length. He had been training doctors in Rwanda and Congo for several years when both countries were enmeshed in civil wars. He was also involved in building a hospital in Congo under the Doctors on Call for Service Foundation. Eithne Keegan was also present and would lead the Congo trip. An RN by profession and an evangelist by calling, she had been to Congo and Ukraine. Eithne became a friend and mentor.

I joined a group of five nurses to provide continuing education at a hospital in Goma. We aptly called ourselves Nurses on Call for Service. Initially, we were planning to go in April 2003 but had to cancel the trip because of civil unrest. We postponed it to November 2003. According to the US State Department, it was still unsafe, but we went anyway.

Our team got together at a restaurant three weeks before the trip. We were excited as we shared our progress.

A young man was sitting nearby. He came to us and said, "Do I hear you correctly? Are you going to Congo?"

We were glad to talk to Tony, a twenty-seven-year-old marine working at Camp Pendleton and attending SVCC. He announced that he would be coming with us!

I said in jest, "Are you sure? We are leaving in three weeks; it will cost you $3,000, and we will be gone for three weeks. Can you remember that?"

Tony was serious. The following Monday, he asked for his vacation time and paid for the trip.

While we were in Congo, we lived in a guesthouse hosted by Dr. Joe and his wife, Lynn. An armed guard was on duty around-the-clock. Tony and the house guard went with us everywhere. They both carried visible firearms, and they kept us safe. I have not been afraid to go back to Africa ever since. God proved to me that He would provide for my safety.

There are other precautions needed before traveling to Africa. You should be in relatively good health. My mentor, Eithne, is an exception to the rule. She suffers from multiple chronic health conditions for which she receives excellent medical care at home. However, the mission field represents additional stressors that put her at risk. Eithne assumes these risks. That makes her very exceptional.

You must prepare yourself for the climate prevailing in the region and bring an entire supply of your medication regimen. In addition, at least two months before your trip, you should consult with your healthcare provider regarding recommended immunizations particular to the area and a prescription of anti-malaria medication since it is endemic in Africa. Having prepared well for the trip will help but not guarantee an uneventful experience.

Departure Time!

With Eithne at the helm, the six of us, Muriel, Graciela, Dawn, Tony, and I, gathered at the Los Angeles airport in November 2003, four hours before our flight. We prayed because we were concerned about our excess luggage. The steward extended *carte blanche* when we explained that the reason for our trip was to share our nursing knowledge with our peers in Congo. God is ever-present.

Here's the trek: Los Angeles to London, ten hours; seven-hour layover; London to Nairobi, Kenya, eight hours; layover, three hours; Kenya to Kigali, Rwanda, an hour and a half. Our hosts sent two vans to meet us, and the ride through the Rwanda countryside took four hours.

Rwanda is a beautiful mountainous country with gardens that occupy every inch of the ground up to the very top. People were standing on the slopes, isolated from each other, looking in front of them like statues, silent, as if they were in shock or lonely. Rwanda went through a traumatic event in 1994 when more than one million people died at the hands of their fellow citizens. People do not trust each other anymore, as many are lone survivors of the genocide.

Reaching Congo through Rwanda

The night soon descended upon us, and I fell asleep while resting my head on Tony. It was the first and last time I experienced such luxury since I often travel independently. Even so, it was not a comfortable ride. Transport in Africa can be challenging. Vans are often old and noisy; the seats are stiff, and the suspension is nil.

We arrived in Goma at 11 p.m. and stopped at the border. The agents asked for our passports, which we reluctantly surrendered when we heard they were keeping them! Congo does not have a good reputation for safety. When we arrived at the guesthouse, Dr. Joe and Lynn reassured us about our passports. They would send the driver to pick them up in the morning after the day shift had a chance to examine them. The story ends well. We got our precious documents back timely.

The Mission Unfolds

While I was on the plane, I read an article detailing the work of Dr. Robert Walley from Newfoundland, Canada, a university professor. Dr. Walley founded MaterCare International, a group of obstetricians/gynecologists and midwives who care for mothers surrounding birth, primarily in the developing world. The article referred to the care required to repair obstetric fistula, which the mother suffers from after a long labor or injury.

When we arrived in Congo, Lynn asked if we knew how to help these patients. Six months earlier, when we intended to travel there but had to delay because of severe internal conflicts, warriors sexually assaulted many women and girls. The Goma hospital had a whole ward of patients who experienced such trauma. The local doctors did not know how to perform the complex surgeries required. I put them in touch with MaterCare International for the training. Already, the Lord was at work in me, fulfilling His plan, "For we are God's handiwork, created in Christ Jesus to do good works, which God prepared in advance for us to do" (Ephesians 2:10, NIV).

Familiar Grounds

We arrived at the mission compound on the shores of Lake Kivu in Goma, the capital. Lovely English gardens surrounded the house. I noticed that the salt-and-pepper shakers were the same as at home. Hanging outside to dry, I recognized a pair of sheets identical to the ones on my bed in California! God showed me that He cared for all of us, that we were neighbors, after all, only separated by two days' travel. Later on, I realized that Lynn shops at Costco when she comes to California!

They had internet and cell phones. Electricity was a bit sporadic; it was a challenge in the morning when preparing for the day. Breakfast was set up outside by the lake. A gentle breeze made the leaves bristle while a cacophony of birds chirping and singing accompanied our morning outings. The food was abundant and familiar: yogurt and granola, fresh pineapple, ham and cheese, homemade bread and jam, salad and avocado, and delicious coffee.

Our Work Begins

Eithne assigned me to the pediatric ward. I observed nurses changing the dressing on a little girl who had suffered a gunshot wound. After attending several dressing changes, our group of nurses agreed to recommend utilizing less caustic solutions on wounds and medicating patients for pain one half hour before the procedure. We included supportive documentation.

In my rounds, I met a mother breastfeeding her newborn baby. She told me she was hungry because her husband was not available to bring her food. In most African hospitals, the family is responsible for providing meals for their loved ones. I shared my lunch and prayed for her. It is the harsh reality of Africa.

Dinners at the Guesthouse

I had the most stimulating encounters at dinners hosted by Lynn and Dr. Joe. Lynn would invite several community leaders. That first dinner, I met Marie-Alice, a Swiss nun engaged in monitoring the prison system in Congo. Her goal was to prevent human-rights abuses. She witnessed up to thirty prisoners in a small cell; they could not lie down to sleep. The lack of hygiene, inherent in such conditions, was overwhelming.

Garret, an aviator for Mission Aviation Fellowship, recounted some of his trips in remote areas and spotting big game in the wild, roaming the vast savanna. It reminded me of the movie Out of Africa. It was fascinating! As long as you are a missionary, you can reserve his services.

We met with counselors for victims of sexual abuse. Recently, a man assaulted one of them because he learned that she was involved in helping victims. Undeterred, our guests were leaving the next day for a trip to the area. We prayed for these brave women.

Lynn had several purposes in mind when she invited representatives of different organizations. It provided her guests with the opportunity to explain their work and mission and find supporters. They could work together to resolve problems that would be intractable for anyone to tackle on their own. It helped prevent isolation and discouragement while allowing them to join in prayer. I have enjoyed these dinners so much that I will implement them myself in my future guesthouse.

Doing What We Came Here to Do

We taught a series of classes. Muriel was uniquely qualified to minister to rape victims. She has a PhD in counseling, a strong faith in the

Lord, and is full of wisdom and compassion. We all found our niches and could accomplish what we came to do and yet so much more. Muriel and I did not know each other before the trip. She became such a good friend afterward.

My presentations were: AIDS/HIV prevention, the relationship between breast cancer and hormonal contraceptives and other factors such as abortion, and an introduction to the Billings Ovulation Method. My audience was very receptive and asked excellent questions. The average attendance was fifty-five participants. I often answered questions for one hour afterward. As required, I provided written papers for all my classes. Since I speak French fluently, I could communicate directly with all the participants. It was a wonderful experience.

Visiting an Orphanage

We visited an orphanage in Goma. Since the civil war, many children have lost their parents and relatives and witnessed war atrocities. There were a hundred children, ages one to twelve, living in a large compound surrounded by a garden and a few wood cabins. One couple, Prospere and Jan, provided for their care. A group of local widows cultivated the garden and ensured a supply of beans, rice, vegetables, and fruit. There was a hut in the middle with a large pot of beans on the fire.

Prospere built a school for the children in collaboration with Doctors on Call for Service.

We toured the cabins. I was incredulous as I noticed no beds and no mattresses or mats. Children slept "shotgun style": on large wood rectangles with dividers. The roof leaked when it rained; the children had no blankets or clothing other than what was on their backs.

I was sitting down speechless, holding the only baby, age fourteen months. I was not ready for this visit. We found the children happy, well nourished, playful, smiling, and singing Christian songs. We joined them. I discovered that God was supernaturally caring for them, and He comforted me with His love and providence.

The Pastor Wannabe

I noticed a chapel under construction and decided to visit. I had to cross a large field with not a tree in sight. I got unbearably hot as I do not tolerate heat well. That is why this call to Africa was strange to me. I was born in Canada; God made me wonderfully—but for the cold! I would go ice-skating at minus twenty degrees Fahrenheit. I kept my windows open at night, even in winter. I asked myself, "What am I doing here?" Even so, God and I have an understanding. I simply said, "Lord, it's too hot for me. I'm going to faint!" A breeze came out of nowhere.

As I continued walking, I came upon gigantic lava stones in front of the building under construction; they were black and shiny with sharp edges. Congo had experienced a volcanic eruption just the year before. A little girl was walking barefoot on scorching rocks. I could not take it, so I cried.

I took in the chapel with its slanted tile roof and outside walls—just a frame. I conversed with the workers in French. What a gift to me, this additional language! A well-dressed young man held a Bible and prayed in front of the chapel. He approached me and said he wanted to become a pastor. I gathered that he had been an evangelist for five years. He requested my help to fulfill his mission. I was aware that SVCC had an outreach for pastors from all over the world. We exchanged email addresses.

This man thought that God would make a pastor out of him if he stood outside a church long enough! I started crying as I prayed for him. The next day, I met Earl, a visitor at the hospital and pastors' teacher. He announced that he was coming to California in three weeks to visit his daughter, who lived in Oceanside, fifty miles from where I lived. We agreed that I would bring him to SVCC, which I did. I also put him in touch with my wannabe pastor.

Spending Time with Nurses

Nurses made up the majority of the staff who participated in our classes. For the most part, they were male, with a ratio of seventy-five to twenty-five. Men are engaged in the workforce, while women attend to their many children. Lynn wanted to start a home-health agency specializing in chronically ill patients. Since home care was my specialty, Eithne asked me to provide some guidance.

Two nurses and I went to visit a man who had AIDS. After evaluating his needs, his nurses made dietary and medication adjustments. The wife and the patient belonged to a support group. The eldest daughter had dropped out of school to attend to her siblings.

I asked the patient, "What about her? Did she know anything about the illness, and was she getting any support?"

I recommended giving her respite time to get together with her peers. I suggested that the parents include her in the decision-making regarding the children.

On our way home, the nurses talked about the Billings Ovulation Method. They liked it very much.

Lynn had invited leaders from other organizations to discuss the start of a home-health agency. She asked how each one could contribute to meeting the needs of AIDS patients in their homes. I answered many questions and offered guidance. It seemed surprisingly easy to start a new service because they did it privately as they combined their meager resources to address pressing issues.

Two days later, Lynn invited AIDS patients to give their input. The patient we visited in his home gave positive feedback. He said he had gained weight, following his nurses' advice. He thanked them for their compassionate care, expressed hope for the future, and gave glory to God. He added that it touched him deeply that nurses came from California to help the African people.

Prayer, a Way of Life

I got close to the nurses. I learned that they work very long hours. They were on call twice a week. Here is what this means: work from 8 a.m. to 1 p.m.; then from 7 p.m. to 7 a.m.; then from 8 a.m. to 5 p.m. When not on call, they work from 8 a.m. to 5 p.m. Nurses complained that their hours were too long and without breaks. I shared their plea with John, their head nurse. How do they deal with it? They pray; the same for the patients. They sing hymns together every morning and evening.

Doctor Joe is an orthopedist. Before any operation, he asks his patients to pray for him and ask God's permission to touch their bodies. He explained that God created human beings in His image; therefore, when the doctor touches the body, he or she is in contact with God's image and creation. Dr. Joe tells the patient that God will do the healing. Afterward, he prays with his patient. Since the doctor has been doing this, his infection rate has been nil. Doctor Joe credits God.

Lynn is a great woman of God. She works long hours, coordinating Doctors on Call for Service ministries, hosting guests, and managing staff. Lynn often drives on crowded roads full of lava rocks making for bumpy rides while suffering from the heat and pollution. She does it all without a word of complaint. She is a great inspiration to me.

The Angel in the Yellow Raincoat

We returned home safely and timely. One incident occurred at the airport in Kigali, Rwanda. I had no luggage to check in. A man wearing a yellow plastic overcoat stood by me. Ten minutes later, we started walking to the gate. The man took my carry-on and started walking beside me. I said, "No, thank you, I will carry it." I did not have small bills; therefore, I could not give him a tip. I arrived at the bottom of a double flight of stairs, not automatic. I started up, carrying my heavy cargo. When I got to the top of the stairs, my heart beat wildly, and I was out of breath. The man in front of me came from Villa Park, California, practically in my backyard! He was kind and concerned and watched me closely while I recovered.

Then we took a van that would lead us to the plane. When I got out, the man in the yellow coat grabbed my luggage and pushed it up the ramp, then gave it back to me. Once I got to my seat, I knew I needed help storing my carry-on. I was about to ask when the flight attendant came and said my luggage was too big to fit in the overhead bin. She took care of it. Once we got off the plane, I asked for my luggage. An attendant said it would come on the carousel. Tony overheard the conversation and said he had seen my luggage on the plane; he ran back to get it.

Upon reflection, I understood that God had an eye on my luggage because He knew it was too heavy for me, especially at a high altitude, more than 5,000 feet in Kigali.

"For your Maker is your husband, the LORD Almighty is His name" (Isaiah 54:5a, NIV). God had made provisions for it all along. God asked me to do what I could. He takes care of the rest, as He proved many times during this trip.

PART 2
A MEDICAL
MISSIONARY IS BORN

Chapter 3. Cutting My Teeth on the Mission Field

> Therefore go and make disciples of all nations, baptizing them in the name of the Father and of the Son and of the Holy Spirit, and teaching them to obey everything I have commanded you. And surely I am with you always, to the very end of the age.
>
> Matthew 28:19–20 (NIV)

Eithne asked me to accompany her to Uganda and Kenya in January 2007. We attended a planning session hosted by Pastor Bruce Sonnenberg, the founder of an HIV ministry called He Intends Victory. Pastor Bruce was the pastor of the Village Church in Irvine, California. We met several times and discussed the work we would be engaged in, the cities we would be visiting, and the precautions we needed to take. I found that spiritual preparation is even more important than the mental, emotional, and physical aspects.

One's going on a mission trip can be unsettling for family and friends. My son, Steven, accompanied me to the Village Church, and he met my team. He gave me a parting gift: a braided necklace with a cross. Steven said, "Mom, please wear it every day," which I did.

The twenty-seven participants came from all over the US and from different walks of life: pastors and their wives, nurses, a medical doctor, teachers, a scientist, and a loan officer. A few had AIDS, and most were already involved in the HIV ministry.

I kept company with Claire, a nurse and coworker. Claire and I walked into the Los Angeles airport, each carrying a heavy bag, when Claire uttered, "Wouldn't it be nice to have a cart?" But there were none available in the restaurant section. As we walked a few feet, we ran into an empty cart. The Lord had provided one right away.

On the planes, I enjoyed an aisle seat; I was restless and unable to sleep except for short naps. It made it easier to stretch my legs and get some exercise. After an eight-hour bus ride, we arrived in Fort Portal; I was exhausted. It was a grueling journey—forty-two hours from home to the hotel doorstep. I have learned to travel since then and take better care of myself.

I slept to the sound of people partying in the hotel bar and the Christian songs and preaching, which punctuated a revival meeting in the neighborhood for most of the night.

Our Ministry Begins

The team visited the local government hospital in Kabarole. We spent the morning touring the wards with Dr. Richard, a young Ugandan doctor. We talked about family planning, and I introduced him to the Billings Ovulation Method. He shared that couples have large families in the countryside because together, they engage in agriculture, which accounts for 85 percent of their national product. In the cities, couples are more likely to consider family planning because they feel crowded. It was a good insight.

We discussed polygamy, marriage at a young age, and the rising incidence of HIV, all prevalent in Uganda. HIV incidence in the general population decreased from 21 percent to 6 percent after a successful ABC campaign promoted by the government. The acronym stands for "*A*bstain from sex before marriage, *Be* faithful to your spouse, and use a *C*ondom if you can't do otherwise." Other African countries focused on condom use but without success. Dr. Richard is concerned that the incidence has risen to 14 percent. He attributes it to married or cohabiting couples having more than one partner; he indicated that polygamy is a factor.

Eithne taught infection control, while I gave a quick overview of the Billings method. The nurses were shy to discuss this subject, and I had to be very sensitive but persistent. Dr. Evelyn Billings used to say that every woman should understand the signs that accompany fertility.

We went to the wards to pray with patients and families. I met Zena, a fifteen-year-old girl with abdominal pain. I asked her if she needed prayer, to which she replied, "I want Jesus to come into my heart." So, we prayed for her salvation. Claire and I moved on to the pediatric ward and visited a baby affected with malaria, her parents being at the bedside. I gave the child a stuffed doll and a trinket. Mom was so delighted she hid her face, laughing. The child needed a blood transfusion, but none was available.

Interestingly, as I walked to the hospital that morning, I met a Jewish nurse working at a Catholic healthcare center. I asked her about any particular need she had encountered. She said no blood was available because no one could process it at the blood bank. Therefore, Claire and I felt equipped to pray for the child, for God had given us understanding.

The Balm of Gilead

We divided into four groups on Sunday, each going to a different church. My team went to Kichwamba Technical College in Kasese District; it was located at the foot of a mountain neighboring Congo. We soon learned about a horrible tragedy in 1998. The Allied Democratic Forces (ADF), a group of soldiers from Congo, came to the school and kidnapped students to supplement their army. The students barricaded themselves in a classroom. Undeterred, the ADF burned the school. More than a hundred students died that night. Our group visited a memorial on the site. Our hearts were heavy when we joined the church service.

Approximately sixty students, primarily young men, listened and responded to a pastor preaching the Word, Pentecostal style. He was a dynamic speaker, and I felt the Lord's anointing. Pastor Bruce had appointed a team member to address the congregation. The Lord started giving me a message outline based on Proverbs 5:5–21, which the pastor touched on. I was not scheduled to speak but told the Lord I would if invited, even though it would be emotional.

The preacher asked us to introduce ourselves and share briefly any message we may have for the congregation. My turn came to speak, and I was not ready; I was shaking inside, which was unusual for me. I barely said two words. I began crying uncontrollably and sobbed for several minutes. They started singing while I was pacing the floor and receiving the comfort of the Holy Spirit. I had never experienced something so powerful. Jesus was healing my wounded soul, and I was experiencing the balm of Gilead (Jeremiah 8:22).

I finally delivered the message and invited these young men to remain faithful to their wives and save their lives. I shared that HIV was rising in Uganda because of the lack of faithfulness to one partner. At the end of the service, the attendees came to talk and hug me. I felt that God was using the pain caused by my divorce to minister to others.

Do You Have a Message for Us?

Our bus stopped for a short break.

A young man was sitting there and asked, "Do you have a message for us?"

I said, "Yes, Jesus loves you," and I shared the gospel.

He replied, "What else?"

I asked his name—the same as my son's, Steven—and I showed him Steven's picture. I shared that we love his beautiful country; we are here to help.

"Be patient; things will improve little by little."

The bus people were calling; I had to cut it short. I prayed for this young man to mature in Christ and be part of the solution.

An Overwhelming Need

The team met with two government officials as part of the process to obtain NGO certification for He Intends Victory. The first officer was very skeptical at first, but he warmed up after we expanded on the ministry's purposes. He suggested adding a program to address married people because their HIV rate was rising. It confirmed the need for teaching the Billings Ovulation Method (BOM) in Uganda.

Couples who use the BOM as a method of family planning have better communication and faithful relationships, which explains why there is a rare incidence of divorce among them. Naturally, there is always an exception to the rule.

"Lord, why me? Why did our marriage fail?"

The Lord responded, "The BOM represented that which was good in your marriage. Without it, it would have self-destroyed much earlier."

A Visit to the Orphanage

We went to the Terry Duffy home, an orphanage supported by the HIV ministry; it is located in Kampala and serves children who have lost one or both parents to AIDS. The children were delightful and well-behaved. After they performed several dances and songs for us, we gave them clothes and toys, creating much excitement. As a result of our visit, I provided monthly support to Anna, an eight-year-old who lost her dad to AIDS; her mom, Jennifer (fictitious name), who was HIV positive, cared for the ten children in residence. Jennifer lived in constant fear of getting AIDS. I could not see God taking her away from them. Children had a teacher and a house director, but they also needed a mother figure, someone who would provide the love they craved. Jennifer seemed encouraged by my message after I prayed with her.

Medical Outreach

Our team conducted a medical outreach in a village nearby. More than a hundred families benefited from the HIV ministry. Their welcome was exuberant as villagers ran to the bus, chanting and dancing, while some women shrieked with delight. They accompanied us to a sitting area carpeted by large banana leaves and introduced us to their chief. They treated us to more songs and dances. The leader then clapped his hands and ordered the elders to show us where to set up our wares.

Eithne organized several stations, such as a welcome team, a triage area, treatment stations, and the pharmacy. There was a prayer team and a clothing-distribution group; the dream team provided toys and candies to innumerable children while entertaining them with sports and games. A professional photographer and video team sprang to action. We had met them at the hotel the night before; they were Christian-college students from Australia. I worked with Dr. Kathy, and we focused on the sickest patients.

During four hours, the medical teams evaluated and treated 288 people. Their complaints were diverse but common: hypertension, malaria, fever, diarrhea, aches and pains, coughing, HIV and sexually transmitted infections, hernias, urinary-tract infection, and skin rashes.

Each family received clothing, toys, medications, flour, and sugar. The villagers expressed the same expansive gratitude and excitement as we climbed the bus for the journey back to the hotel. We enjoyed dinner outside after a tiring and emotional day. Several times throughout the day, I caught myself tearing up. Despite their living in profound poverty, I admired them for their courage, gratitude, and joy.

The next day, the team went to another village and conducted an agricultural outreach. They brought farm tools and seeds, discussed farming methods, and distributed flour, maize, beans, sugar, clothing, and toys. Claire and I could not join them because we were feverish and suffered diarrhea. Eithne provided some antibiotics, and we felt better the next day.

Meeting Christ at the Crossing

We arrived at the border between Uganda and Kenya. Our destination was Eldoret, Kenya, a mountainous region in the Great Rift Valley. It took two hours to obtain our visas allowing us to cross over into Kenya. If arriving by air, you must acquire one beforehand.

It looked like a vast, dusty, dry, and hot plain with nary a shred of vegetation.

During our crossing, Claire and I led six young boys to Christ. She prayed for Wilkins, John, and Isaac, while I prayed with Alfred, Omar, and Bernard. What a blessing! These youths were selling bananas and drinks. Sixteen-year-old Isaac asked for a Bible; I gave him mine after dedicating it and asking him not to sell it. He carried it around proudly afterward, and I observed him reading it while sitting apart.

Claire and I were concerned because David, our driver, went missing while we were waiting for our visas. When we were ready to depart, he was still absent; so, we prayed. Bernard inquired why. I told him he should pray to God whenever he has a need. He asked if I could pray for his business; "Sure," I said, which I did.

A boy asked for water. Claire gave him her bottle. Bernard quickly grabbed a bottle from his basket and gave it to her. I asked the boys to pray for one another because they were now brothers in Christ. As we were getting ready to leave, and with David having reappeared, we took pictures of our boys to remember to pray for them.

Family Impact

We arrived at our hotel in Eldoret. It was a tall building, and it looked good from the outside. The rooms were very modest, not like previous accommodations. I reminded myself we were on a mission, not a luxury vacation. I was grateful to obtain a fan upon request. There was no mosquito net around my bed, so I prayed, "Surely He shall deliver you from the snare of the fowler and from the perilous pestilence. He shall cover you with His feathers, and under His wings you shall take refuge" (Psalm 91:3–4a, NKJV).

Sandra, a travel companion, was sick; Eithne went to care for her.

We visited Tom and Ellen, a wonderful couple in charge of the Family Impact ministry. They are involved in marital and HIV counseling, abstinence, and life-skills education. Tom has a theology-and-counseling degree; Ellen is a midwife.

Next, our group visited thirty street kids living close to a pile of rubbish. Many sniffed glue to stave off hunger. I became distressed when I noticed a naked toddler walking in the rubble. A young couple with us, Steve and Sarah, wanted to rent a house and take these children off the street. In minutes, we gathered $400 between us as seed money for their new ministry under Family Impact. They quickly bought blankets and bread. Before we parted, we prayed for this young couple.

A Visit to the End of the World

We left for Nakuru, still in the Rift Valley, halfway from Nairobi. The bus ride was challenging. We were cramped; the roads were rocky, dusty, and arduous, and the traffic was dense.

I came down with severe nasal congestion. I took frequent sips of water to prevent the congestion from settling in my lungs. The bus was chugging wearily along as it climbed one hill after another. We prayed it would not stall, overheat, or blow up a tire.

We stopped in Marigat, a village nestled in the mountains with hot, dry, swirling dust and nearly a shred of vegetation. I was feverish, dehydrated, and weak. Villagers were expecting us, and we met in their church. Ellen had asked me to introduce the Billings Ovulation Method. I looked and felt horrible; she left it up to me, but I would not miss the opportunity. As I was sitting next to Pastor Jim, I asked him to pray for strength. I was crying, just asking him. I heard myself being introduced and made my way to the front.

With the help of an interpreter, I shared how women can learn to recognize their fertility by observing one sign. The couple can then decide to come together during the fertile time to achieve pregnancy or avoid that time to postpone it. I tried to use simple terms. I told them about Drs. John and Evelyn Billings and how they knew that the method could help in the fight against HIV because its practice helps the couple to remain faithful to each other. I was able to speak loud enough and with authority. I ended with greetings from Australia and California, telling them that the Billings wanted to touch Africa and that I was there on their behalf, having made that commitment in 2005. I told them their little village represented the end of the world, or all the world, because of the area's remoteness, perched as it were in the mountains of Africa.

It's Only Thirty-Five Km Away

We got back on the bus. No matter how many times we asked him, our guide would always say it was only thirty-five km away. Pastor Bruce had decided we would spend the night at Crater Lake in Naivasha. For the last ninety minutes, I asked for a pit stop many times. The place was so remote there was no resting area. I said I would go in the bush, but there were signs on the road, "Caution, wild animals crossing."

We arrived at the Crater Lake lodge around 9 p.m. We were exhausted and grumpy as we settled in our little cottage hidden in the woods and furnished with narrow bunk beds—a camping-like experience in my book. Surprisingly, I did not suffer from belly pain due to bladder overextension, and, with Jesus at my side, I fell asleep despite my nasal congestion.

Eithne and I woke up to a delightful display of bird songs. When we stepped outside, we were a few feet away from the lake where pink flamingos were waddling. Our group went on a short nature hike with a safari guide. Bruce had surprised us; we were in a game sanctuary. He asked the driver to take us on an expedition where we encountered elegant giraffes, muscular zebras, delicate gazelles, elands with their intricate spiral horns, and imposing colobus monkeys. After lunch, we left for the Nairobi airport, as our flight was departing in the evening.

Forever Meeting Our Needs

Claire scratched her leg when she got off the bus. Because many were HIV positive in the area, she worried that her wound would get infected. The day before, I had found two antibiotic ointment packets in a bag of toys. I was about to discard them when I thought it would be wiser to put them in my purse. Claire was so relieved when I pulled out the medicine. Josh noticed a splinter on his foot at the airport and needed the same. God delights in being there for us.

Our trip back to California went well; the logistics of getting twenty-seven people on the same page, luggage and all, is evidence of God at work. Pastor Bruce did his part by planning our trip carefully. I arrived on a Friday and was back to work two days later. By then, I felt as good as new, except that I noticed a few more wrinkles; it takes its toll!

It was a fantastic trip, an unforgettable experience that filled me with gratitude toward God for calling me to serve Him and the African people in this way.

Chapter 4. Signs and Wonders Will Follow Me

Very truly I tell you, whoever believes in me will do the works I have been doing, and they will do even greater things than these, because I am going to the Father.

John 14:12 (NIV)

In January 2008, I joined the same team for another trip to Uganda and Kenya. We visited Dr. Richard at Kabarole Hospital and discussed my desire to open a medical clinic in Uganda. He suggested I locate it in an area where there is a lack of specialized medical services. I discussed HIV with Jollie, a clinical officer, somewhat equivalent to a nurse practitioner or physician assistant in the US. She studied 200 pregnant patients who came to Kabarole Hospital for prenatal care. In March 2006, 86 percent of this group tested positive for HIV, a massive infection rate.

The Future of Africa

During our first medical outreach and as we were setting up, I prayed for the young men in the community. As I walked to my area, I met a group of men in their twenties who would act as interpreters. I told them that God had laid on my heart to pray for them. I encouraged them to build good houses, be faithful to their wives, and care for their children and families. I reminded them that the future of their community was on their shoulders and that God would help them.

Doing the Work God Called Us to Do

I participated in three medical outreaches. Dr. Kathy and I cared for a very sick child affected by malaria. We visited the Terry Duffy Home in Kampala and HIV support groups—the purpose of the HIV ministry. We canceled our trip to Kenya because of a terrorist coup at a mall.

Pastor Bruce sought NGO status in Uganda. We met with government officials for approval. I asked Bruce if I could take a day to investigate my work in the region, and he gave me his blessings. While attending the NGO meeting, I spoke to Dr. David W., the department-of-health-services director. I requested an appointment with him to discuss my desire to start a maternal/child health clinic under Alliance for Life International. I gave him our brochure and showed up at his Jinja office two days later.

Dr. David W., trained at UCLA in California, introduced me to Dr. Sarah B., a public health deputy officer, and I explained my purpose.

Dr. Sarah asked, "Do you want to work in a hospital as a nurse?"

I answered, "No, I want to provide upgraded medical treatment in maternal and child health."

Dr. David W. continued, "There is a small hospital in Buwenge, run by Dr. Daniel L., a born-again physician. Would you work as a partner with him to upgrade the facility and equip it to provide cesarean sections?"

I said, "Yes, that would be great."

Dr. David W. introduced me to Mr. Semei, a Buwenge clinical officer, who came down to meet me and take me to the hospital immediately if I were available. I turned down public transportation and chose to go by *boda* (motorcycle) with Peter, a young man I had met upon arrival. It felt like living an adventure all the way. David, the hospital manager, was expecting me, and we toured the facilities. I took detailed notes and several pictures, which guided me throughout the upcoming months in planning for the upgrades. I communicated with Dr. Daniel L. and involved him in setting priorities.

Back in Kampala, we stayed at Emmaus Guesthouse, owned and operated by Fields of Life, a UK ministry. I had a fascinating conversation with Phil, who managed a charity in the UK and had several projects in Uganda. He was married to a nurse. I shared my desire to start a project in Uganda.

Phil gave me two analogies that characterized his charitable work; the first one, he called, "Here I am; signs and wonders follow me." Phil explained, "As long as I am walking, signs and wonders follow me. When I stop, signs and wonders also stop" (based on John 14:12). He went on, "Ugandans have to do the work eventually. You must disciple them. Then they should take over." Phil brought up his second analogy, "Picture a wheelbarrow; we take each a handle, a Ugandan and me, and we push. It goes well, and the work advances. When I go away, the work stops; little progress is made, but it will get done little by little."

I recognized godly wisdom and felt as if God was meeting and preparing me for the work we would do together. "The LORD possessed me at the beginning of His way [...]" (Proverbs 8:2, NKJV), "And He is before all things, and by Him, all things consist" (Colossians 1:17, KJV).

On my way to the airport, I had two prayers for Uganda: "Please, Lord, bless Uganda with a clean and economical source of power for vehicles; Lord, please provide electricity for the medical centers, especially for that little hospital of mine in Buwenge."

Later on, I added, "Lord, I will sit with whomever You want me to sit on the plane; please choose my companion."

On our way from Entebbe to Dubai, with a stop in Addis Ababa (Ethiopia), I was sitting next to a young man from Germany. I asked about his destination and purpose. He was going to Addis Ababa for a four-day conference with African leaders. His job was to provide solar power to medical centers in Uganda, financed through the World Bank. He was involved in more than 400 locations but not in Jinja yet.

Then I showed him the pictures of the Buwenge facility. We looked at the lab picture, and he recognized batteries run by solar power; they were used to power the fridge in that room. He said that the staff connected other things to the battery and that was why it might not work as it should. With the zoom option, he was even able to determine where these batteries came from. He was interested in the Buwenge hospital because it is a health center 4 and in better condition than the ones he had visited. We exchanged information, and he promised to look into my little hospital in Buwenge.

I was in awe of God and how promptly He had answered my prayer, and I realized that signs and wonders shall follow me...

Chapter 5. The Work Begins with Heartache

> Be alert and of sober mind. Your enemy the devil prowls around looking for someone to devour. Resist him, standing firm in the faith, because you know that the family of believers throughout the world is undergoing the same kind of sufferings.
>
> 1 Peter 5:8–9 (NIV)

I returned to Uganda in August 2008 to begin our work under Alliance for Life International. My friend Alexis, with whom I served in the Salt & Light Ministry at SVCC, came with me.

Are We Really in Africa?

We spent the first night at the BOMA, a guesthouse owned and operated by a couple from the UK. We loved their quaint cottages, English gardens, and the best breakfast in town. In the morning, Godfrey, our travel agent, came to meet us. When I entered the main lobby, I saw a young man dressed in safari beige pants and a collared black T-shirt, trim haircut, tall and slim. I had met Godfrey on a previous trip to Uganda, but I had not recognized him from the back. He was working at the reception desk on a wireless laptop computer while using his cellphone. Jokingly, I commented that he looked very American to me!

The Sign of the Cross

We went to Africa Renewal to set up our visit with John, Alexis's sponsored child. Even though the process started in the US, it was best to appear to further our purpose. Africa Renewal's building is on the shore of Lake Victoria in Kampala. As we were leaving, we noticed the sky was cloudy but with a small patch of blue. It formed a cross. In my spirit, I felt that God was pleased with their work.

Great Reception: the Bats Are Out in Force

Godfrey drove us to Jinja, forty-four miles from Kampala. This town of 300,000 people is famous for its electric dam. We went to the Brisk Hotel Triangle, located on the shore of Lake Victoria, and observed the sunset from the rooftop. Uganda is on the equator, and sunset is at 7 p.m. Many birds were coming out of the trees, circling above us, and going back to their nests. We realized many were bats; they live in palm trees. You recognize them by their constant chirping. There are few mosquitoes in this area because bats feed on them. Mosquitoes are a threat in Uganda as they carry parasites that cause malaria. We came to like the bats.

Surveying Our Work before We Begin

We started with the laboratory: a broken fridge powered by solar. Electricity was available in the hospital but sporadically. They had a generator outside that was supposed to be activated when this occurred. However, there was often a lack of fuel to operate it; therefore, nurses used flashlights.

Outside the lab, several patients were sitting on the grass, waiting in turn. They held a weekly AIDS clinic at the hospital. Mr. Semei pointed out that many patients got weak in the hot sun. He recommended a covered patio with benches. We visited the operating theatre, which they used rarely. It needed lights in the ceiling as they only had a floor lamp. Mr. Semei noted that windows should be opaque and closed to provide privacy and prevent dust.

The operating room was a stand-alone building. United States Agency for International Development (USAID) built it in 2000. The intent was to use it for tubal ligation and vasectomy; both procedures render a person sterile. Despite much education regarding the perceived need for these services, the population refused them. The donor did not equip it for other surgical procedures, and it stood unused. Once a month, an ophthalmologist did cataract surgery using the floor lamp. Occasionally, a clinical officer would use it for suturing a wound.

Mr. Semei echoed the Jinja Department of Health Services. There was a need to equip this room for a cesarean section, as it would save lives. The staff referred women in obstructed labor to the regional government hospital in Jinja, twenty-three miles away. The journey took at least forty-five minutes. The mother in labor required evaluation and often had to wait for the doctor to perform the cesarean section. To save the lives of the mother and child, the doctor must operate immediately. Mr. Semei pointed out the lack of a covered walkway between the main hospital building and the operating room. At this time, it would be challenging to push a gurney on the grass from the labor-and-delivery room to the theatre.

We visited the hospital wards. We found that foam mattresses were very thin, soiled, and torn, with no available pillows or bed linens. The patients brought their own or lay on the bed fully clothed. Hospital gowns were not the norm. The mother occupied the crib with her sick child because there were no chairs available. The paint was peeling, especially from the metal bed frames. There was a deep-water well on the grounds, which provided clean water, and it was available in the wards. The hospital staff lived in housing units on the grounds' periphery. It was part of their salary and helped with staffing.

We agreed that painting hospital wards, including the furniture, providing new mattresses and bedding, and painting the four buildings outside, would be our top priority. It would improve morale and provide a cleaner environment before we equipped the hospital for major abdominal surgery. We met Inja, who was in charge of volunteers, and scheduled the work to begin.

Alexis and I distributed medical supplies, children's clothing, toothbrushes, and crafted dolls. Receiving the gift of brand new clothing is a rare occurrence in Uganda. The gift came from the Council of Catholic Women, a St. Nicholas Church ministry in Lake Forest, California. My sister Michelle from Canada provided the dolls, which occasioned so much joy.

Mr. Semei accompanied us to Jinja, where we bought painting supplies. Back at the hotel, we wished each other a restful weekend and planned to meet at the hospital on Monday morning. Alexis and I reflected on our first workday and encouraged each other: we did everything with much efficiency and purpose. We showed up; we were not overwhelmed, and they took us seriously.

Leisure Time

Early Saturday morning, Alexis captured a gorgeous sunrise while taking tons of pictures with her sophisticated camera. In the afternoon, we took a boat ride on the lake. Our guide showed us the different bird and tree species, a fantastic variety. He explained that the Nile River, which is 400 miles long and reaches Egypt, originates from Lake Victoria. He brought us to an island where we could see the end of Lake Victoria with its quiet waters and the beginning of the Nile River, as evidenced by turbulent currents.

Back to the hotel for dinner, God blessed us with our very own bird show, crows flying in pairs and diving in front of us, turning over, and even fighting in the air. Alexis finally got her stork picture. It had not moved from its perch on top of a cutout palm tree. I prayed she would get to capture the bird in flight. Morning and late afternoon, she waited immobile and at the ready. Just as I decided to leave, Alexis got her picture, God's reward for her patience.

The Work Begins with Heartache

Alexis and I reported to the Buwenge health center 4 on Monday morning, anxious to begin painting. A group of teenagers, young children, and a few women gathered for prayer. Alexis intended to surrender her camera to David, the hospital manager, for safekeeping. As she was hurrying to put it in its case, it fell to the cement floor. The lens broke, and part of it caved in. Alexis was devastated and blaming herself. Sadness enveloped us.

Our Scripture reading that morning began with, "Praise be to the God and Father of our Lord Jesus Christ, the father of compassion and the God of all comfort" (2 Corinthians 1:3, NIV). We prayed that God would minister to Alexis. She had also brought a small camera. The kids kept her busy all day, taking pictures of them. She was smiling and happy. However, at the end of the day, she was still blaming herself. I said to Alexis, "It was an accident. I could have done it. Would you forgive me? Could you forgive yourself, Alexis?"

We started with sweeping the ward and moving the furniture outside. The volunteers began sanding the metal furniture to prepare each piece for painting. Then Ibrahim showed up, a painter by profession. He took over from that point on and came back every six months for the next two years, each time working for ten days, doing all without remuneration. Usually, I would give him school fees, for he had seven children.

Attending the AIDS Clinic

After observing the progress we were making with painting, I joined Charles, a clinical officer in charge of the AIDS/HIV clinic. More than 1,000 patients required monthly assessments to check their blood count and obtain their medication supply. I pointed out that nine out of ten patients were women. Charles explained that men die first because they do not come for care, or they wait until they are very sick. The women learn they are HIV positive when seeking prenatal follow-up or care for other conditions. The patient then starts on antiretroviral drugs to arrest the progression of the disease.

Charles was very kind, compassionate, professional, and knowledgeable. I asked how he came to this line of work. He lost two brothers to AIDS, both doctors.

Our Last Day in Buwenge

After eight days at the hospital, participating and supervising the painting operations, taking numerous trips to Jinja to buy bedding and paint supplies, including a trip to Kampala to acquire mattresses, it was time to say goodbye. Alexis drew five murals while the teenagers painted accorded to her outlines. Every time I tried to participate, a volunteer would rush toward me and start doing the task. Everything turned out beautiful.

Mr. Semei, Dr. Daniel, and the community showed up, including a reporter. Alexis gave dresses to the volunteers, cookies, coloring pages, and crayons to the children, and I gave Ibrahim a tape measure.

We thanked God for bringing His work to completion. It turned out to be a beautiful plan that God used to build the community while offering mentoring opportunities for young people and giving hope to everyone. The reporter asked, "Why Buwenge? Why not Jinja?" They did not see themselves as deserving, but God did.

Visiting Our Sponsored Child

We set off for Namutamba with Godfrey, and we picked up Samuel along the way. Samuel is a social worker representing Africa Renewal. The journey was long and arduous at times as there were many un-paved roads on this hundred-mile expedition.

We visited with Fred, who was in charge of the project, which bene-fited 230 children in the area. Village women had prepared lunch for us: potatoes, chicken, liver, coleslaw, avocados, and chapati. I was afraid to eat uncooked food, but I decided to pray and accept their gracious offering. It was delicious and well tolerated.

After visiting the school, we headed for the bush. We found the brick house overlooking the valley and marveled at the magnificent views. Cultivated gardens, mango trees, a tea plantation, chickens, and goats roaming around completed the idyllic setting, so it seemed.

Samuel introduced us to a ten-year-old boy named John, his twelve-year-old brother, and their grandparents, who were elderly. We learned that the boys' father died of AIDS and that their mom went to live in the city. They never saw her again, for she probably died of AIDS.

We visited the house that grandpa built. It had several rooms and a sturdy roof, an outside toilet, but no flooring or furniture. Grandpa talked about the need to finish the house but said he had run out of money. Alexis had brought several gifts, including a few straw mats. Grandma danced around the courtyard, delighted with this gift. She explained how difficult it was for her to sleep on the ground because of hip pain. Alexis and I held romantic musings regarding their living conditions. Seeing grandma's reaction to a simple floor mat jolted us back to reality. Alexis vowed to order two beds and send them through Africa Renewal. We concluded our visit with pictures and prayers.

An Unforgettable Safari Experience

Alexis, Godfrey, and I set off for the Mweya Safari Lodge located in the Queen Elizabeth National Park. We stopped by the equator crossing, a famous landmark.

Winston Churchill called Uganda the pearl of Africa.

We discovered the land's riches: most luxuriant vegetation, green valleys, snow-peaked mountains, dense forests, tea plantations, and herds of cows.

Lake George and Lake Albert surround the lodge. An impressive elephant sculpture greets you on the grounds at the main entrance. The main lobby is vast and furnished with elegant English-style furniture, high back upholstered chairs, wood furniture, tile floors, and carpeted areas. The butler welcomed us with refreshing passion fruit juice. After we visited our room, we headed to the patio and ordered lunch: shrimp salad with avocado and tuna and a glass of Chardonnay. I could have been in California, but no, I was deep into the savanna surrounded by wild animals, including lions! Yellow little birds kept perching on our table, making sweet chirping sounds and welcoming us.

In the late afternoon, we left for our first safari with Ben, our guide. He asked us what animals we would like to see. I quickly answered, "Lions."

Ben said, "If you're lucky, you might see them."

I responded, "I prayed that God would give us favor with His most majestic creation."

Ben replied, "You still need luck."

I am not sure if I said it out loud or to myself, but it went like this, "You may trust your luck, but I will trust my God."

Finally, after driving more than one hour across fields of tall yellow grass, bushes, umbrella trees, and herds of antelope, the lion's favorite prey, we spotted a big lioness lying on the meadow, in quasi-perfect camouflage. There were three more lions in the distance, but we concentrated on the one close to us. We wanted to take pictures of her, but she would not budge. We finally drove around her, ever so slowly. She finally got up and walked around while we clicked away. The other lions never drew closer. We saw elephants, water buffaloes, antelopes, and wild boars on our way back to the lodge.

Alexis and I had dinner in an elegant dining room while selecting from an exquisite menu. In subsequent trips, guests enjoyed buffet-style dinners with delicious food in abundance. We woke up early the next day to join a safari before dusk. Several guests met in the main lobby, sipping tea and eating small muffins. We parted with our guides and drivers, some in vans or SUVs and some in the actual safari vehicle, the famous open jeep where passengers can stand and take pictures unencumbered. There was palpable yet subdued excitement and competition between the safari participants: Who would get to see the most coveted big game in the wild? On that safari, we saw warthogs, giant forest hogs, buffaloes, spotted hyenas, antelopes, elephants, waterbucks, gazelles, and a leopard, but the lions were missing in action.

Meeting Abraham, the Pool Attendant

After enjoying a buffet breakfast, we lounged around the pool, where I met Abraham, the pool attendant. He asked about my religious affiliation when I said, "God bless you" in Luganda. Abraham inquired if I had any Christian literature. Alexis quickly gave him a Bible. I learned that Abraham goes home weekly to visit his wife and newborn baby. The young couple had lost their first baby, born full-term after extended labor. She really should have had a cesarean section, but it was not available. This time, Abraham chose a White hospital where his wife had this planned procedure for the second baby. This encounter confirmed the need for an operating room to accommodate this type of surgery at the Buwenge Hospital.

As we were exchanging information, it brought up the subject of my divorce, which was still very painful to me. On this trip, I found it challenging to meet new people as the conversation would often bring up marital status. I had just read that suffering is a transition to happiness, a ray of hope for me.

A Safari Cruise

We went on the channel between Lake Edward and Lake George for a safari cruise. We saw crocodiles, a hippopotamus, African Cape buffaloes, giant lizards, and a herd of elephants. We learned to recognize several bird species particular to this area, including egrets, herons, pelicans, and majestic eagles. Back to the lodge before dinner, we had time to refresh before enjoying another culinary experience in the bush.

God Offers Second Chances

On the third day, we stopped at the hotel gift shop for last-minute shopping. They had a great selection of African art. Alexis was intent on taking more pictures as we were leaving the park. Godfrey had worked on her damaged camera and was successful in making it usable for the time being. Now that her fancy camera was working, God gave her several opportunities to take great photos of animals that she had only seen from afar during the last two safari expeditions. They came right up to the road. Some assumed their most attractive stand, not flinching for several minutes until Alexis had taken pictures from all angles. God has a touching sense of humor and justice.

It may be that having her powerful camera handy while at the Buwenge Hospital would have been intimidating and distracting. Ugandans, in general, do not like to have their picture taken by strangers. It is advisable to ask permission. As for the children—they love it.

We drove back to Entebbe and stayed at the BOMA guesthouse. It is a great way to end the trip, relax by the pool, and enjoy the gardens before traveling back to the US the next day.

Chapter 6. God Saves Baby Angela

My frame was not hidden from you when I was made
in the secret place, when I was woven together in the
depths of the earth. Your eyes saw my unformed body;
all the days ordained for me were written in your book
before one of them came to be.

Psalm 139:15–16 (NIV)

This time, my aunt, Micheline, accompanied me in February 2009.
Until I retired in 2013, each of my trips to Uganda lasted seventeen to
nineteen days. A typical itinerary went like this: three full days of travel; nine to eleven days are devoted to the main project; the last two or
three days include travel and teaching the Billings Ovulation Method.
There is usually an opportunity for a three-day safari, especially when
it is my guest's first trip to Africa.

We arrived in Buwenge two hours later than expected. Everything
takes longer than anticipated. Africans do not have the same sense
of time as Americans. Many do not own watches, although business
people often do. Paved roads are two-way; they are often full of giant
potholes. A twenty-mile ride on such a road takes forty-five minutes.
In this first encounter, we got lost. David, the hospital manager, Dr.
Daniel, Nurse Christine, and Charles, the clinical officer, patiently
waited for us. This time, we plan to paint the remaining wards in the
first building, buy mattresses, repair many broken windows, and install
fluorescent lights. Upon leaving the hospital, Dr. Daniel insisted that
we use their vehicle and driver from now on, and we would pay for
the fuel.

The next day, we visited with Dr. Sandra, director of the department of health services (DHS) for the Jinja District. We explained the purposes of our trip. Dr. Sarah was very professional, helpful, and engaged in facilitating our work. We met the district electrician, who accompanied us to the hospital to assess the work needed.

After buying paint and supplies, we arrived at the hospital as the volunteers headed by Inja were washing the walls. We found out that the floor lamp and the generator both needed repair. Paul, a local building contractor, came to estimate the walkway and the windows. David indicated he would find a supplier for the mattresses and bedding.

The God of All Comfort

I noticed a teenager in labor sitting on the grass. Her two sisters and her mom were standing nearby while the patient was suffering in silence. I introduced myself as a visiting nurse from the US and asked if I could sit next to her. I sat behind her as she was contorting herself in obvious pain. I asked her to lean on me as I rocked her slowly and prayed for her. She was thankful for the attention. When I got up, I asked her relatives if they could take turns sitting behind her since she was not in a bed. Later on, I walked by and noticed her sister holding her.

A Surprise Visit

Micheline and I were planning a Sunday afternoon boat ride but we had to cancel it because of inclement weather. We witnessed a discussion between the hotel tour guide and Godfrey as they rescheduled. Micheline was impressed with their promptness and communication.

Mr. Semei called to announce his visit. Micheline remarked he was probably coming to discuss business. Mr. Semei came with his daughter Seesee to pay his respect. They gave us pineapple and sweet bananas. Everyone has been so kind and appreciative of our collaboration.

Baby Angela

Back at the hospital, we met Charles, the clinical officer. He was distraught. He had lost his third brother, a forty-five-year-old man suffering from hypertension. I prayed for Charles.

Then a woman named Adilla came bearing a newborn baby in her arms, accompanied by her son. He explained that she had found the baby girl the night before as she took a walk in her neighborhood. Someone had left a baby girl swaddled in a blanket by the side of the road. Adilla picked her up and called the police to report the incident. They accompanied her to the hospital, where the nurse examined the child and determined she was in good health. The police officer allowed Adilla to keep the baby. The son asked for financial help to enable Adilla to assume care for the child. I offered to look for a sponsor in the US and gave her the first monthly installment. My friend Muriel, who came to Congo with me, sponsored the child.

We later found out that baby Angela was born to a teenage mother at the Buwenge health center two nights prior. It brought back to mind the young woman in labor with her relatives by her side. It may be that she is the mother. God placed Adilla on their path and provided an adoptive mother for baby Angela.

The Work Continues

Ibrahim, Inja, and the young people are working very hard. We met with Dr. Sarah at the DHS in Jinja. We discussed a partnership between the Alliance and their department to allow us to finish the work sooner. Dr. Sarah explained that the current budget did not allow it. She also shared that the government was planning to build a new hospital in the same region, therefore precluding further significant improvements at the Buwenge facility unless privately paid. I was disappointed but found comfort in prayer.

Several visitors came trolling throughout the day. Someone requested reading glasses. Alexis had given me some before I left on my trip, so I was able to help. Agnes, the speaker of the Jinja District, came to thank us for the work and invited us to a town-council meeting. Some council members came to express their appreciation and provided lunch for the painters.

A Gift from God

I met with Joseph (fictitious name), an HIV counselor and laboratory assistant at the hospital. He shared that he had been HIV positive for the last fifteen years. A few months ago, he came down with tuber-culosis. His wife was also HIV positive, but not their four children. There is a very high success rate in preventing HIV transmission to the newborn if the treatment starts timely. They announced the birth of their fifth child, a two-month-old baby girl. I offered my congrat-ulations. He replied that she was a mistake. He confessed he should have known better than to risk for her to be HIV positive. I felt sad that he talked about their baby as a mistake.

I told him this child was born out of his love for his wife. I continued, "She is a gift from God, the same as every child, even if born in diffi-cult circumstances."

Edward reacted by saying, "Oh, I'm so glad. I will tell my wife."

A Flow of Gratitude and Always More Needs

Our last day in Buwenge brought feverish activity. Dereck and his crew were completing six murals. Another team was applying a sec-ond coat; women were cleaning the floors. We got the last bid for the windows. Many visitors came: the Buwenge town council, the district secretary of health, the hospital chairman, the town clerk, and the Jinja District speaker. They were bearing gifts: a plaque, T-shirts, and food for the volunteers.

The hospital chairman insisted we go and visit the new Boise health center 2 in Buwenge, where they do thirty deliveries per month. They have one labor-and-delivery table, one set of delivery instruments, and two beds lacking mattresses. The midwife, Randy, asked me to sign the visitors' book. She was pleading, and no doubt praying, that I would agree to fund the purchase of furniture for the center. I did not make promises but took pictures and assured her that I would share their needs with our supporters.

I met with David, Nurse Christine, and others to give detailed parting instructions. We felt that if everyone knew what was happening, it would provide accountability and decrease the risk of mismanaging funds. In subsequent trips, we followed the same process and never had improper use of funds.

Teaching the Billings Ovulation Method in Jinja

The World Organization Ovulation Method Billings (WOOMB) informed me that they had already introduced the Billings Ovulation Method in Uganda. In 2009, I met Fr. Patrick in Jinja. He was the senior pastor at Lady of Fatima Church and an enthusiast Billings supporter. He introduced me to Nurse Dorcas and midwife Harriet, who had traveled to Australia to attend teacher training. Fr. Patrick shared his desire to hold a teacher training in Jinja. They now had several couples who were using the method successfully. It had changed their lives for the better.

Teaching the Billings Ovulation Method in Rakai

We got together with Samuel and his wife, Edith. Samuel is the social worker who facilitated our visit with Alexis's sponsored child six months prior. He would like me to teach the Billings Ovulation Method in all the villages where Africa Renewal has established schools, churches, and health clinics.

We met with Godfrey, our driver, Samuel, and Micheline in the lobby of our hotel in Kampala. Samuel was distraught. He told us he was not successful in securing a car for us to go to Rakai. His employer did not want to pay for it. He was so disappointed, but it was a misunderstanding. We already had a vehicle and a driver. Through this experience, Samuel realized that he wanted to have his own project. He showed interest in our desire to start a pregnancy resource center once we completed the Buwenge project.

Rakai is close to the Tanzania border. When we arrived, there were 115 people waiting for us in the church. Men asked pertinent questions, but women were not so inclined. We provided extra teaching for breastfeeding women afterward, and the pastor invited us to come back in August.

Teaching the Billings Ovulation Method in Kampala

Samuel invited me to teach the method to twenty-six couples from his church, a more educated crowd. They were skeptical but warmed up as the teaching progressed. A couple said they had been using the method for eleven years. They encouraged others to try it and support one another. Their pastor would like to become a teacher so that he can bring this knowledge to villages. The woman who is using it led us in prayer to spread the Billings method in Uganda. The pastor followed suit and prayed for my health, longevity, and safe travel. God used this show of support to help me spread the Billings Ovulation Method in Uganda.

Chapter 7. God Calls Us to Do More

For we are God's handiwork, created in Christ Jesus to do good works which God prepared in advance for us to do.

Ephesians 2:10 (NIV)

Good News and Bad News

In August 2009, Dr. Daniel came to pick me up at the airport. He told me, "Louise, I have good news and bad news," then, he announced the start of a three-year specialty degree in obstetrics/gynecology. Therefore, he would no longer be the doctor at the Buwenge health center. I rejoiced over his choice of specialty. He would make such a difference in the care of mothers.

We stopped by his house in Kampala and visited with his three young children. His wife, a pharmacist by profession, had returned to work. They lived simply on his $300 per month salary. In the US, this would be a power couple. Upon program completion, he plans to work for the United Nations or a major NGO because they offer better pay. As a pro-life advocate, I commented that most organizations would be involved in promoting abortion. The issue never leaves my mind. Upon graduation, Dr. Daniel worked in South Sudan and now works at Mulago Hospital in Kampala, affiliated with Makerere University. He is making a tremendous difference in the care of women and their babies.

Things Are Looking Up!

David, Mr. Semei, and Ibrahim welcomed me back to Buwenge. The grounds were free of trash, and the hospital wards were clean. We discussed painting the exterior of the buildings and our work for the next nine days.

Equipped with a load of painting supplies, Mr. Semei and I showed up the next day, ready to work. More than a hundred patients were gathering between the buildings. An organization from the United Kingdom was conducting eye examinations and providing glasses. Nothing was custom-made as in the US. Even so, some would see better for the first time.

Ibrahim was preparing the walls for painting; he expected his crew to be available the next day. The students were arriving home that day for a three-week vacation. Most went to boarding schools. As a former English colony, Uganda modeled its public education system after the UK. I realized that I could not have been planning my trip better than to arrive just when the students were coming home on break. I had to request my vacation time from work months in advance. I am thankful that God is always in the mix.

God Calls Us to Do More!

Mr. Semei and I went to visit the Boise health center. Midwives Sarah and Mr. Semei's sister, Aleysa, welcomed us warmly. The facility was still bare, like last time. They needed beds, mattresses, bedding, benches, chairs, tables, desks, a medicine cabinet, and one surgical instrument kit for delivery.

When we returned to the US after our first trip in August 2008, we planned a garage sale. My friend Joy, a long-time coworker in the Salt & Light Ministry at SVCC, said she would come to help. She is always the first to show up.

When Joy asked for time off, her employer inquired, "A garage sale, for what?"

Joy explained, "It is to support the work of Alliance for Life International in Uganda. They are involved in equipping a small hospital to perform cesarean sections; this would help save the lives of mothers and babies surrounding birth."

Joy had a famous boss, Jan Crouch, Trinity Broadcasting Network founder and president of the Smile of a Child. Jan gave us a generous donation of $10,000, which she repeated six months later.

I found that God finances His work. Naturally, as the president of the alliance, I am responsible and directly involved in fundraising. Ultimately, He is the one who touches people's hearts and makes sure the right person hears about the work in some way, somehow. In all those years coming to Uganda and maintaining a pregnancy resource center, we have never run out of money. We rarely have a surplus, either. It is like the manna in the desert. God only sends what we need to cover immediate needs. God wants us to look up to Him and trust Him, for "God is able to bless you abundantly, so that in all things at all times, having all that you need, you will abound in every good work" (2 Corinthians 9:8, NIV). I am so thankful for our supporters, a small group of faithful servants who are sharing in the work.

More Good Works

Besides the main objectives I plan to accomplish in this brief period, there is a whole layer of charitable work with its own rhythm. I am the only *muzungu* (White person) for miles around except for the UK organization, which is here for only one day. My continued presence invites inquiries. I do not want to turn anyone down. I make one exception: when a young, healthy-looking man asks for help, I usually say that I am focused on helping mothers and children. I pray that God only sends those He wants me to help and that the amount requested will make sense. It is working out that way.

I visited with Jessica, David's wife. Jessica showed me the gently used sewing machine she bought with the $100 gift my aunt Micheline gave her last time. Jessica needs an electric converter so she can use it, which I will provide. Jessica would like to open a sewing shop in town. I asked her to gather information on the rent and the cost of fabric. I try to support independence.

Praying for Rain

Back to the hotel after a full day's work, I felt so blessed to be involved in this type of work. At the town-council meeting in the morning, I learned that the rainy season had come and gone without a drop. All were concerned for their crops because the drought had already damaged their first harvest. I said I would pray for rain, and I invited the city leaders to join me.

Breakfast brought relief, a fine but continuous rain that lasted forty minutes. We drove to Buwenge, where I met Paul. The men had started digging for the walkway. The ground was hard and dry, making it difficult to dig. There were mounds of rocks and cement nearby, and Paul explained how to make the walkway. A man came to me looking for work, and I told him I would inform the supervisor. Paul said the man working in the trenches was drunk. I told Paul I did not like this. The man could hurt himself or others with the pick. I told him about the man who was looking for work. I let him deal with the situation.

The men were hard at work painting the main building. I went to get lunch for them and got caught in torrential rain. People were thanking God and rejoicing.

Baby Angela and Her Family

Baby Angela delighted us with a surprise visit. She was six months old, a little small for her age, but she was tiny at birth also. She sounded as if she had bronchitis, a frequent occurrence here. I provided the monthly sponsorship, and her sister Aisha asked for school fees. She remarked that her family was not able to survive on their meager income. Adilla does not speak English, so Aisha continued, "We are seven people in our family. Adilla buys jackfruit at the market and resells them." They lived in a large brick dwelling with a good roof but unfinished inside. It was dark and humid. Angela's crib was in a room by itself; there were a few single beds, a sofa, and chairs. They owned a plot of land down the road, but it remained uncultivated.

I asked Aisha to talk to her mom and develop a plan to increase their family income.

"Would Aisha and Shakira like to learn how to sew?"

Jessica would be willing to train them.

A few days later, Aisha shared their plan: "We would like two goats, a male and a female, some hens, and a cow. May we also get maize and bean seeds?" Her sister Shakirah would like to become a tailor, and Jessica agreed to teach her. I congratulated them on their thoughtful planning. I said the cow was not possible at this time. A cow is a great family asset, but it is expensive. Mr. Semei said he would get the goats; Jessica recommended they start caring for the goats first and get the hens later. Aisha shared that her family was very thankful for the help.

Everything Is Getting Done

We are halfway through our stay in Buwenge. Everything is progressing well: the walkway is underway, and the city engineer paid us an inspection visit. He recommended upgrades to meet construction standards. The painters are tackling the exteriors of four buildings. I am constantly reevaluating our expenses to make sure we have enough to complete what we started.

Mr. Semei and I went to order wood furniture, custom-made, for the Bwase health center, at the cost of $600. I am particularly pleased with this transaction. I did not think we would be able to meet their needs, but God showed me otherwise.

We visited Dr. Sarah at the DHS. She gave us a letter to use with customs when collecting the ultrasound machine at the Entebbe airport. Mission Hospital in Mission Viejo, California, donated this life-saving equipment. I brought up a future project. Dr. Sarah hesitated, then said, "I would like to see how this gets utilized first. The improvements you made will appeal to patients; they will want to use their hospital instead of delivering their babies in the field." I liked her thoughtful and straightforward approach.

Mr. Semei, David, and I went to the National Drug Authority in Kampala for the ultrasound clearance. We learned it could take five days; this was not an option. At the airport, I negotiated with the customs agent. It did not matter that Dr. Sarah confirmed she was receiving it. It did not matter we were nonprofit. It did not matter that it was a donation for the Buwenge health center and that it cost us $1,800 to ship it. Nothing mattered. We paid $220 and retrieved it. All along, I was telling myself how this piece of equipment was worth it because it would save the lives of mothers and babies surrounding birth.

We went to the Joint Medical Store and ordered delivery instruments for both health centers, two delivery tables, and two mattresses at the cost of $2,454, or $1,000 less than my estimate. We rejoiced and gave thanks to God.

Our Last Day in Buwenge

Ibrahim and a few volunteers finished the painting. With the added funds I provided, Paul will complete the structural improvements recommended by the engineer. I admired the newly cemented driveway while contemplating its use. I visited Jessica's business, a sewing shop close to the village center. She was proud and hopeful as she looked at her sewing machine and array of colorful fabric.

Angela's family got their two goats and a half, one being pregnant! We feasted on chapati and drinks as they expressed their gratitude. I asked what had changed in their family since they adopted Angela. Aisha shared that Angela had brought more friends: you, a White person who cares for us, and Muriel, the sponsor, whom they call the "European mother." They were radiant and full of hope.

Back at the hospital, Mr. Semei retrieved the ultrasound machine from the truck. He had been gone all morning for prayers at the mosque. He is a very devout man, a great leader, very generous for his time, and always involved in helping the community. He is a father of nine children, married to Aida, his wife of thirty years. He said they are partners as she also works outside the home and contributes to the family's welfare. All their children are getting an education. One son just completed his bachelor's degree in agriculture. Ugandans place a high priority on educating the next generation. Many did not finish high school, but their children go to universities at the cost of enormous sacrifice.

We gathered around the box encasing the precious ultrasound. It was exciting to unwrap it together as we took pictures and discussed its future use. Dr. Sarah was planning for someone to obtain an ultrasound certification.

We met the town health-committee chief, the town clerk, and the Buwenge staff and volunteers. Mr. Semei addressed the crowd, and so did

Michael, David's eldest son. I thanked them for their hard work and encouraged them to remain involved and mentor someone. I shared with them that hospitals in the US have volunteer groups involved in fundraising to improve their hospital. They felt that this experience had changed them. They affirmed that volunteerism was there to stay because now they liked their hospital.

I felt such a sense of accomplishment because of experiencing God's blessing on the Buwenge region. It rained again yesterday. It is at His command that "He raises His winds and the waters flow" (Psalm 147:18b, NABRE).

Teaching the Billings Ovulation Method in Buloba and Rakai

Harriet, the nurse-midwife from Jinja, joined me for a Billings teaching in Buloba Village on the outskirt of Kampala. Samuel and his fiancée Edith came with us. Samuel and I were carrying out our plan to introduce the Billings method in several villages where Africa Renewal was sponsoring children. He had prepared the groundwork carefully so that we were expected and welcomed. There were twenty-five people, most of them women. Harriet introduced the method in an enthusiastic way as she shared anecdotes in Luganda and English.

We provided another teaching in Rakai. We could not get the projector to work, so I used a blackboard and posters while Judith and the pastor acted as interpreters. The questions were all pertinent, which was very encouraging. This time, there was a good mix of men and women. Men were confident and asked many questions—the same type I would get in California. It does not matter if it is an audience of farmers or doctors. I am barely exaggerating! The inquiries pertained to using the fertile phase to achieve pregnancy or postpone it according to the rules of the method. The subject arouses the same level of interest and scrupulous attention wherever I have taught the subject.

Traveling in Uganda

Driving back to Kampala, our driver Badrue asked for prayer for easier traffic. He was tired from the night before since he had given Harriet a lift back to Jinja, a four-hour journey altogether. I prayed as I usually do before each trip. Badrue and I go back to 2007 when I first came to Uganda with He Intends Victory. He is a careful, attentive, and skilled driver, and I feel safe with him. He is a nonpracticing Muslim. Badrue often drives Christian groups all over Uganda and surrounding countries.

Yesterday, he noticed a Bible outside on a table as it began to rain. He said, "The Word of God is getting wet." He quickly grabbed the Bible, put it aside, and gave it to the pastor later on. Badrue has listened to so many prayers. It is bound to influence him. I shared the gospel with him two years ago, but he wasn't ready. Edith is delightful; she will be a good wife for Samuel. Now that they know the method, they are planning to use it when they get married next year.

Teaching the Billings Ovulation Method in Namutumba

Samuel and Edith joined my teaching the next day in Namutumba. We used the projector and the computer without any problem. Samuel joined us as an interpreter. The church staff showed generous hospitality by offering us a delicious meal of matoke, rice, and chicken. Our team is working well together; it is promising.

Future Planning

During our travel, Samuel and I had plenty of time to consider the future of the alliance in Uganda. We discussed starting a pregnancy resource center and, later on, a maternity home. Samuel shares this vision. Abortion is illegal in Uganda; however, it is still frequent and easily accessible. There is a need for services related to women or teens in unplanned and distressing pregnancies. Before my trip to Uganda, I had visited a pregnancy resource center/maternity home in Long Beach, California, called His Nesting Place. Their ministry influenced me greatly.

Samuel recommended that the alliance apply to become a nongovernmental organization (NGO). It is a lengthy and involved process that will bring recognition for the work we are carrying out in Uganda. Samuel is familiar with the process; he will guide us until we achieve it. We discussed a location for our center. I liked Jinja; Edith and Samuel preferred Kampala, a modern city. We decided to continue to seek the Lord's guidance.

A Restful Day before Travel

The weather in Entebbe is lovely; a gentle breeze cools the air and creates a perfect ambiance. I walk in the manicured gardens, rest on a nearby bench, and call everyone I worked with during this trip. I thank them for their support and bring everyone up to date. This time I connected with Dr. Charles, Fr. Patrick, Mr. Semei, David, Dr. Daniel, and Paul. We are doing meaningful work together for a time. I lift them to the Lord so that He may continue to care for them in every way. I know that when I am back in California, a different life will captivate me. I will be visiting loved ones, returning to work at the hospital, and catching up with administrative duties.

Chapter 8. Spreading Our Wings

In a desert land he found him, in a barren and howling waste. He shielded him and cared for him; he guarded him as the apple of his eye, like an eagle that stirs up its nest and hovers over its young, that spread its wings to catch them and carry them on its pinions. The Lord alone led him; no foreign god was with him.

Deuteronomy 32:10–12 (NIV)

Buwenge Is Calling!

I came by myself in February 2010. Upon arrival in Buwenge, David praised Paul for doing an excellent job with the walkway and mentioned he needed some prodding to complete it. Fred, the town engineer, had submitted plans for new bathrooms as requested. We met with the town council and shared our plan to provide air conditioning in the theatre and a covered sitting area next to the lab. We requested a bid for the sitting area.

We moved on to the Bwase health center, where we met Sara. We admired their new furniture, as it was sturdy and well built. David pointed out they needed a small fridge to store medications.

Back at the hospital, I observed Nagakolo, their head nurse, as she was attending to pregnant women and taking their blood pressure with the equipment we provided. I was delighted to hear that they came every month, starting with the third month. Next, Nagakolo and I admired the two new labor-and-delivery tables. They were in need of a suction machine and additional BP cuffs and stethoscopes.

I met with Paul, our contractor. He confessed that it was not easy to work with the town council when I left in August. They were up-set they had not gotten the contract for the walkway. They felt they could have done a better job. Paul explained that younger people are supposed to defer to their elders. I had obtained a bid from the Jinja District engineer, but he was asking for $500 more. I preferred Paul, an experienced Buwenge contractor who would hire local people. I checked the walkway, and it looked acceptable to me. I told Paul he was in the running for the sitting area. Fred, the Buwenge town en-gineer, would submit his plan to Paul. Then Paul could offer his bid. I told Paul to include timelines for completion and stick with them.

Fred and I met separately to discuss his bid for the bathrooms: three toilets, three showers, one sink, two large water tanks, and a replen-ished septic tank for $3,800 after a 10 percent discount. I told Fred I would go with him for the bathrooms since the work was more com-plex. As for the sitting area, Fred said he must act as the quality con-trol supervisor if Paul gets the bid. He played that role already for the walkway. Fred said he would not charge for the plans as they repre-sented the town council's contribution.

More Good Works

I met with Jennifer, a widow and a mother of three sons. On her mea-ger housekeeper salary, she could not afford school fees. I extended a donation for school fees and $50 for two female goats.

Joyce was a nursing assistant. Her husband was diabetic and unem-ployed, and they had five children. I asked her to develop a plan. After consultation, Joyce requested one male and three female pigs, which I provided.

Christine was the head nurse. She was divorced and had three boys. There was a new addition to her household, a fourteen-year-old girl relative. The boarding school had accepted the teen girl and was re-questing school fees. Christine needed $100, which I provided. She wanted to manage a canteen on the hospital ground, but the starting cost for inventory was too high.

Jessica and I discussed her sewing business. After one month at that location, rent was due again. The property owner asked for a year's rent; this was not unusual in Uganda. She was back at home and giving sewing lessons to young girls. Their three oldest children were applying for college grants. We prayed for school fees, an ever-present concern.

I visited with baby Angela and her family. She was recovering from malaria and a respiratory infection. I gave her a beautiful dress, a gift from her sponsor Muriel. It was a ray of hope amid the darkness. Mom proudly showed the child's up-to-date immunization record. Financially, they were still not making it. I inquired about the plan put in place last time. The pregnant goat delivered twins, but one died. No one seemed to work the garden patch; therefore, they had to buy their vegetables at the market. The hens died. Did that mean they ate them? The young women were not working or going to school, and Shakira did not like sewing.

Adilla showed me the room where she slept with Angela. I noticed the dirt floor, frayed, thin mat, and a single bed in a corner with a torn mattress and no bedding. I said I would help with these items. Later on, Jessica suggested we cement the floor because the room was so humid. It would help cut down on the child's frequent bouts of bronchitis. Paul agreed to repair the leaking roof, cement the floor, build an entrance step and ledge, and change the door hinges, all for $125; he said he would provide free labor.

Fadilah (a fictitious name) was the hospital housekeeper. She had lost her husband to AIDS three years ago. She and her two children lived with her in-laws, but she could not meet the rent; therefore, she lived in constant fear of being asked to leave. I could not get a smile out of her. I offered a child sponsorship for Peace, the six-year-old, and I advanced the money for the next two months. When back in the US, a child sponsor stepped in.

Meeting Dr. D., a Sad Man

David and I met with Dr. D., the assigned doctor for the Buwenge health center. He completed his studies as an ophthalmologist and applied for a position in his field. Dr. Sarah refused. First, he has to work for three years as a generalist as per an agreement to cover his medical studies. Dr. D. is afraid of losing his newly acquired skills in the process. He could not get excited about improving maternal and child health even though I offered to bring an ob-gyn doctor from the US to work with him. We discussed the needs of the Buwenge hospital. When we parted, David, Jessica, and I prayed for him. Subsequently, Dr. Sarah allowed him to work for the state as a specialist instead. God is always in the mix.

Everything Gets Done

Robert, the electrician, came. We negotiated for the air conditioner, including installation and floor-lamp repair. I said no to the floor lamp since it should fall under regular maintenance.

It was time to make our regular run to Kampala to buy medical supplies and the small fridge. Mr. Semei used his last three days' fuel money to wash his car and change a tire before our journey. I found all my drivers very concerned about my safety. We stopped by the DHS office in Jinja and met Dr. Charles. I found myself tearing up as I was recounting all that we were accomplishing for this little hospital. I was in awe of what God was doing through us.

Teaching the Billings Ovulation Method in Buwenge

When visiting with Steven, the Buwenge mayor, and his staff, he asked if I could teach the Billings method in surrounding villages. I was thankful for his interest and promised to address the need. When we moved on to the Bwase health center, the midwife announced that she would assemble nurses and midwives for a Billings teaching during my stay.

Back in Buwenge, as I was distributing supplies and taking pictures for the occasion, a visitor named Ben asked me to come and visit with him and his wife in the children's ward. She was attending to their four-month-old baby, who had malaria. Their eight children ranged from age fourteen years to four months. Ben told me they needed help; they really could not afford any more children. Could I do something for them? The couple agreed that I would teach his wife to recognize when she ovulated. This way, the couple could avoid intercourse during the time surrounding ovulation. I continued, "Would you be willing to abstain from intercourse during that time?" Ben agreed and excused himself because he had to get back to work.

I taught his wife the Billings method using a ruler, a simple way to teach, even if the client is illiterate. She spoke good English and asked appropriate questions. She tried the calendar method, but she got pregnant anyway. I referred her to Nurse Christine for a follow-up. It was such a wonderful experience to have direct contact with the local people.

The time came for teaching the Billings method introduction to ten nurses and midwives at the Bwase health center. I used the new teaching material for health professionals. I could sense they had difficulty grasping the concepts. I learned from this experience and hoped to have the opportunity to reinforce the teaching.

Teaching the Billings Ovulation Method in Kacwungwa and Muleete

We left the Jinja region to go to Kampala. In the darkness, the incoming traffic is always scary to me. The pollution is intense as black smoke is coming out of old vans, called taxis, which carry up to fourteen passengers. Trucks are numerous, and they are the worst offenders. I have learned to accept these conditions as they are integral to my work. I often pray about it, and I have seen significant improvements over the years. In the worst spots, the Lord sends me a breeze as a reminder He is with me. When Badrue is my driver, he puts the windows up when the worst air is present, then puts them down. Badrue maintains this habit even when I am asleep. It reminds me that the Lord's grace is sufficient for me, for His power is made perfect in weakness (based on 2 Corinthians 12:8).

Samuel, Edith, Badrue, and I left the next day for Kacwungwa, a village in the Mubende District. We enjoyed the panoramic verdant valleys as our SUV climbed this mountainous region with no difficulty. We met with sixty people gathered in a school, and I used the blackboard to explain how to identify the fertile phase in cycles of various lengths. They asked several questions. They liked the method and wondered what was next.

The next day, we stayed in the region and went to a church in Muleete, a village nestled in the fertile hills of central Uganda. Parishioners filled the church; they wore elegant apparel, and the itinerant preacher gave a powerful message, "God loves people who love Him back! He is gracious to sinners, and that is how He wins many of them." After the church service, the pastor encouraged his audience to remain in their seat for the Billings teaching. More than 200 people attended. I gave the introduction using a video presentation projected on a large screen. I could have been in California! The group was too large and intimidating for the type of questions we usually get at the end of a presentation. The pastor concluded by saying, "We liked your presentation. Why don't you come back and spend a week with us?"

For the previous two years, I had been creating awareness about this method in many settings. It was time to train teachers. There was a government official in attendance. He encouraged me to spread knowledge of the method.

Visiting a Pregnancy Resource Center/Maternity Home

Samuel and I discussed his budget for our pregnancy resource center (PRC). We visited a PRC in Kampala. We met with Vivian, the founder and director. She opened her center five years ago and received referrals from all over Uganda. Only one US donor finances it. The center accommodates twenty-five girls. The young mother returns to her family once the baby is two weeks old. If her family is unwilling to receive her, Vivian finds a suitable family to host the mother and child. We find that this PRC/maternity home will be a good resource for our teenage clients. This way, Samuel and I can concentrate on opening the PRC.

God Opens a Door

Back in Entebbe for my upcoming flight the next day, I go for a walk in the neighborhood. As soon as I sit on a bench at St. John's school, teacher Moses joins me. After learning about the alliance's work in Uganda, he invites me to speak to their students. I report to the classrooms the next day and talk about loving God and doing their best in school and at home while I invite questions. A girl says she wants to visit California; another one wants to go to China. With the primary seven children, I discuss how to discover God's gifts and their life purpose. The true meaning of life is found in God and serving others. I pray with each group, and then Moses whisks me away to meet Steven, the school principal.

The principal asks pertinent questions as he seeks to know me better. When I share that the alliance plans to start an NGO and a pregnancy resource center, his mood darkens. I ask Moses why and he responds furtively, "This is a taboo subject. Teenage pregnancy is the fear of every principal." Moses intervenes and shares that the alliance focuses on prevention. I explain that our program is age-appropriate; we involve teachers in selecting the presentation. For example, middle and high school students may learn about a healthy view of human sexuality in the context of marriage, prevention of teenage pregnancy, and sexually transmitted infections by emphasizing abstinence of sexual activity while unmarried. Principal Steven seems reassured and asks us to share our curriculum with him. We exchange contact information, and I promise to get in touch with him when I am back in California.

Moses gives me a tour of the grounds. He points out that there are fifteen- to sixteen-year-old students even in a primary school as there are fluctuations in attendance and inevitable delays. In the 1950s and under British rule, they built these facilities for British students. After Uganda achieved its independence in 1962, the government repurposed it as a public school for Ugandans. It accommodates 700 students, of which 200 are boarders. The school is in disrepair; there is only one flushing toilet; they use outhouse facilities instead. The children planted trees on the periphery; tempting avocados hang from a nearby tree; banana and orange trees abound.

It is lunchtime. Workers bring large metal containers filled with maize and beans. Excited children quickly form a winding line while school staff serves the food. We stop by to see the teachers in their lounge; then, we are off to visit Moses's family.

I meet his wife, Elizabeth, and four of their seven children, aged three months to six years. We take pictures, and I tell them about my tour of the school. I plan to keep in touch with Moses, our point man. We marvel about what God may have in store for us as we collaborate on this vital matter.

Back at the guesthouse, it is time for a quick dinner as I leave for the States in the evening. There is a long flight pattern awaiting me, but I always welcome it. I know that I will be reflecting on all that we accomplished during this eighteen-day journey, the beautiful people I met, the deepening friendships, and the new opportunities to serve. I am anxious to get back to my adult children, Steven and Caroline, renew contact with my friends, resume my work as a nurse case manager, and advance the alliance's purposes. In short, I am ready to get back to my other life in California!

The Rwanda Connection

The first leg of the trip from Entebbe to Amsterdam is an overnight flight. My neighbor's name is Amal (fictitious name), a Tutsi from Rwanda who lives in London with his partner and their eight-year-old daughter. He does not trust the future enough to get married, "It is good for now; who knows in the future." He lost his parents and three brothers in the carnage. Amal learned that his sister had survived, and he was looking for her. He works as a newspaper deliveryman even though he comes from a wealthy family, decimated at this time. He has been to Belgium, where he met some Hutus, the offending tribe. Amal comments, "Water under the bridge; spilled milk; no one can remedy." He is trying to move on with his life.

What do you say when you hear such a tragedy? Amal seems to be living in a state of suspended animation. How do you rebuild your life when your loved ones died violently while you were powerless to stop it and even had to flee to preserve your own life? You barely exist because the event shattered your trust in humanity. You miss your loved ones every anniversary, every holiday, every time you come home and would like to share life's happenings. Only God can heal his broken heart. I resolve to pray for Amal, for emotional and spiritual healing, and for God to help him find his sister.

Chapter 9. No License— No Operation

Everyone has heard about your obedience, so I rejoice because of you; but I want you to be wise about what is good, and innocent about what is evil. The God of peace will soon crush Satan under your feet. The grace of our Lord Jesus be with you.

Romans 16:19–20 (NIV)

Travel Worries

I was back in Uganda in August 2010. Most of my airline trips to Uganda had been uneventful, but not this time. I was so excited to welcome Dr. Ross, his wife, Shirley, and their friend, Nurse Theresa, whom I met through a technical exchange in Christian healthcare. Dr. Ross is an ob-gyn, a pastor, and a seasoned medical missionary. He built a women's clinic in Haiti, providing safe deliveries in an impoverished area. They live in Missouri, where Shirley manages a local medical clinic for the poor, where they both work. Nurse Theresa lives in Illinois; she is in charge of a nonprofit medical supply store, a resource for medical missionaries.

We had different itineraries and airlines. The airline canceled their first flight due to poor weather; they missed their connecting flight. They were dealing with aviation companies with neither assuming responsibility. They spent a night in Brussels. It took Theresa six hours to rebook a flight; she succeeded, but it had to be in first class. Initially, the airline offered a flight for August 10. Strangely enough, this was supposed to be the date they were to leave Uganda, not arrive there.

Finally, they landed in Entebbe after a sixty-six-hour journey. They were grateful to see me there in the middle of the night with our driver

Michael. We spent the night at the BOMA nearby, an oasis for weary travelers. After a refreshing swim in their beautiful new pool, followed by a delicious and hearty breakfast, we went to Jinja and enjoyed a boat ride on the Nile River. It seems that God was making it up to us.

Our Work Begins

We met with Paul, the contractor, and Fred, the city engineer. We sat on the newly built covered patio, the fruit of their labors. There were no more patients sitting on the grass: we are making progress!

We gathered around with the operating room (OR) staff. During the next four days, we would deep clean the OR and adjacent rooms, every nook and cranny, in preparation for using the theatre for a cesarean section if the need arises. We were to prepare and sterilize instruments, use the suction machine, verify their anesthesia and oxygen equipment, and ensure cleanliness. Dr. Ross got everyone super motivated.

Nursing students, housekeepers, and our team joined the OR staff in the task. Dr. D. was a no-show. He is supposed to work closely with Dr. Ross to learn how to perform the procedure. Dr. Ross was protective of him. He wants to use the OR even if their doctor is unavailable.

We visited with Dr. Sarah at the DHS. She announced her promotion to the Ministry of Health as quality commissioner. I reflected that I would be losing her for our work in Jinja. She said, "Louise, you are gaining a friend at the Ministry of Health!" In Uganda, you can get a lot done based on your relationships.

The luggage finally arrived five days later. Dr. Ross was very thankful and said he owed me *meat on a stick*. It is an inside joke as it refers to barbecued meat sold on the street to car travelers. He knows I do not trust the source. I responded, "I prefer to celebrate the first cesarean section with a bottle of champagne!"

Dr. Ross was assembling two complete instrument sets out of the four available. The OR crew was ironing uniforms to prepare them for sterilization. Dr. Ross set up the ultrasound and tried it on our first patient, Juliet, who was at term and in labor for her first child. We all gathered around as Dr. Ross showed us the markers he was monitoring. He was so pleased to discover that the ultrasound had OB software. We all learned that it was a boy! In this traditional culture, there is more excitement surrounding the birth of a male child.

Dr. Ross announced that everything had to be ready for surgery the next day in case the need arose. There was a flurry of activity to sterilize the instruments. There was only one problem; Dr. Ross did not have a medical license to practice in Uganda. We started the process three months ago. The Ministry of Health staff assured us it would be ready when we arrived in Uganda. Since we reached, I had been calling every day to resolve the issue. I finally asked Dr. Daniel to intervene, and he got through. There was only one signature needed, but the person responsible was away for four days, and no one else would step in. Dr. Ross was blaming himself, "I should have parked myself in Kampala and not budge until I got my license."

I said, "It's the council's fault for lack of professional courtesy, same for Dr. D., who only showed up for a couple of hours today after we have been here for one week." I continued, "You came here at great cost to yourself to train a doctor and staff in a life-saving procedure."

Dr. Ross was anxious to use the refurbished theatre and work with his crew. Shirley must have intervened: no license—no operation. Even though Ugandans are not litigious, we should not risk such an outcome. I prayed that the need would not arise to force the issue. We hoped the midwife could refer the patient timely to the regional hospital in case of protracted labor.

Theresa taught infection control to thirty-six nursing students and staff while Dr. Ross presented the care required surrounding surgery. Soon, the world learned that there was a *muzungu* doctor in town offering a life-saving ultrasound exam. From two women on the first day, his customer base expanded exponentially. Nurse Christine assisted Dr. Ross in performing ultrasound exams on pregnant patients while Theresa and Shirley kept the patients coming. Theresa and Dr. Ross gave another class, this time on obstetric care, and the staff did well on their test. Shirley had prepared several prizes. She was quiet and unassuming, yet things ran smoothly around her.

The Good Works Resume

As soon as I sat on the new patio, villagers kept coming. Dr. Ross called me "Queen Louise" for our humanitarian work. Uganda is a Commonwealth nation, so his allusion is appropriate. My prayer went like this, "Lord, bring only those You want me to minister to out of our budget." I had reserved a $500 fund. It was significant for us but a drop in the ocean of need.

Nurse Christine asked for school fees for her fourteen-year-old niece. She lived with her mother in the village, along with several siblings. Her uncle wanted to marry her off, but her mother refused because she found her daughter too young. The uncle called Christine twice a week to get the girl back. Christine was at a loss. The teen watched the kids while Christine was at work. She was crying as we discussed her situation. She did not want to go home but desired to return to school. I gave school fees, and we prayed while the girl made the sign of the cross and found peace. David and Christine planned to meet the family and discuss what was best for the child.

The Child Who Needed Surgery

Jennifer, the housekeeper, requested school fees for Gerard. She referred me to Aminah, an eight-year-old girl who lived with her grandpa. He earned a living by repairing plastic jerry cans; they typically contain forty pounds of water. You find these containers throughout Uganda, as most homes or huts do not have piped water. He charged five cents for repair. A pittance. How could anyone survive on such a meager income? Many have garden plots that they cultivate. Otherwise, they would starve.

The child came with her grandpa, and Nurse Christine acted as nurse and interpreter. Aminah was seen at the Jinja Regional Hospital and scheduled for surgery to care for a bone infection. She was not going to school because of arm pain. Grandpa did not keep the surgical appointment because of the cost. I immediately knew where this was going and uttered a quick prayer, "Oh Lord, please do not let it be more than $50." It was such confirmation when the grandfather said that the Jinja hospital requested that amount for the surgery.

After the procedure, Aminah will come to the Buwenge hospital daily for six weeks to receive an intravenous antibiotic. Grandpa agreed with the plan. We prayed for Aminah as we were all excited to see God at work.

The Gift of Light

Paul invited me to visit his business in Buwenge. It is also the seat of a nonprofit organization that he cofounded. They teach young men and women the skills of carpentry, upholstery, and sewing.

There were sixty people in attendance. The women were cutting patterns sitting on the floor while two of them hovered at the machines. There was no light and no window in that room, so I decided to offer them a gift of light. They also presented me with two small tables, handmade and engraved with the name of the Alliance. Their organization invites people from other countries to share their construction skills and bring tools. They have only a couple of hammers for forty men. In subsequent newsletters published by the alliance, I shared that opportunity. So far, I have not been successful in meeting the need. Even so, they persevere despite severely limited resources.

A Miraculous Fall, a Gift of Friendship

Paul had invited me for lunch after the visit to Joppa Carpentry. I had to stop by the hospital first. I left the theatre in a hurry and missed a step. I fell hard on the dirt with protruding metal bars just next to me but only sustained a scratch. I quickly dusted myself and went to Paul's house, shaken but grateful to be unharmed.

Prussia, Paul's wife, and his sister Eunice had prepared a delicious meal for several people. Not everyone is comfortable eating in people's homes in Africa. Theresa and Shirley had strict diets while in Uganda. Ross and I pretty much ate everything. Prussia was fasting for a Muslim ritual. There are many Muslim people in the region. Uganda is 42 percent Catholic, 42 percent Protestant, 15 percent Muslim, and 1 percent Animist, and they get along well.

Paul asked me to pray. We enjoyed a delicious meal of potatoes, rice, beef stew, vegetables, and avocado. Paul gave me green apples to share with my friends. It was a precious time, and Paul and I experienced a deepening friendship.

Sharing the Gospel with Our Neighbor

Across the street from the Buwenge health center, there is a private hospital serving the Muslim community. I had the opportunity to visit when I first arrived in the region. It is equipped for deliveries and cesarean sections.

Dr. Ross had asked me if I would maintain a relationship with Samir (fictitious name), their hospital administrator and a Muslim.

I said, "Yes, I believe the best Christian witness is to befriend them."

Dr. Ross added, "We also need to share the gospel with them."

Samir came to visit, and Dr. Ross shared the gospel with him. He said, "Samir, when a Muslim who lives in Egypt changes his religion, they kill him. What would happen in Uganda if one were to change his religion?"

Samir did not hesitate and said, "Nothing."

So, Dr. Ross said, "What are you waiting for, Samir?" And Dr. Ross prayed for him. A few days later, Dr. Ross gave him an extra set of instruments for a cesarean section. Samir was so grateful because they only had one set. It was an excellent way to cement the relationship with our neighbor.

A Parting Gift

It was our last day in Buwenge. Mr. Semei thanked us for the work and assured us they would keep the theatre very clean and in good order.

George, the town health commissioner, came and commented, "You did everything you said you would do when you came to us in 2008. Thank you so much."

Mr. Semei gave each of us a bundle of colorful African prints.

Visiting the Sick

Theresa had arranged a home visit to a disabled man living in Mpumudde. He is paralyzed from the waist down and uses a wheelchair. His immobility led to a chronic wound to the lower back, which is painful and requires daily dressing changes. Dr. Ross and Theresa quickly assessed his needs: a mattress, bedding, vitamin B, a gel cushion, and a new wheelchair. The team bought the needed supplies and made arrangements for delivery after we left.

Before we departed from Jinja, Theresa invited us to visit a patient in the hospital. The young lady received care at the Buwenge facilities and was referred to the Jinja Regional Hospital for specialized care. The young woman had a late-term abortion at twenty-two weeks and was complaining of abdominal pain. Today, she was going for surgery. We prayed for her recovery.

Abortion is illegal in Uganda. Even so, it is easy to obtain and usually performed by medical personnel. It happens this way: the pregnant woman gets a medication over the counter. The drug is for another purpose, but it starts the miscarriage process. Once the bleeding and abdominal cramping start, she goes to the hospital for a surgical procedure to remove the dead child. It is called post-abortion care. Some doctors and physician assistants coordinate and participate in the entire process. There is nothing wrong with the hospital providing post-abortion care. It becomes an ethical issue when the medical personnel is driving the procedure, which is often scheduled at night to avoid suspicion. I tried to dissuade a medical practitioner when I told him, "Do you want your exceptional skills to be used in the service of life or death?" He acknowledged my concern. I said I would pray.

The Medical License

We stopped by the Ministry of Health in Kampala to pick up the medical license on our way to the airport. It had just become available, ironically, the day Dr. Ross was leaving Uganda. Once it was securely in his hand, I addressed Raoul (fictitious name), the clerk responsible for this poor outcome. I said I was very disappointed with the process because it had come too late for Dr. Ross to participate in surgery as planned. I indicated that Dr. Ross, his wife, and a nurse had come to Uganda at great expense to help a government hospital, and they were met with indifference by his office. The clerk explained that he would reduce the fee for the next time. Now that I have been in Uganda for a significant period and have dealt with government staff and people from other fields, I found that when there is a persistent delay in obtaining a service, it is a way of inviting what they call *facilitation*. I do not participate in this practice. However, if I am asking someone to go beyond their regular duties, I offer compensation.

Dr. Ross was gracious. I observed the same forgiving attitude when he had to wait for his luggage. Dr. Ross is a man of God, a pastor, an evangelist, a doctor, and a humble man. He has kept abreast of our progress over the years. He drops me an encouraging note, like his most recent one, where he told me his men's Bible study was praying for us. I am so grateful and honored to have welcomed him, Shirley, and Theresa to share our work.

Nursing Student Scholarship

Fr. Mubiru asked if we could extend a scholarship for a deserving student. Maria is studying to become a psychiatric nurse, an emerging field in Uganda. There are few health professionals qualified to care for these patients.

Maria shared her grades with me; I found she was doing well, and I liked her. It seemed feasible since she had only one year remaining. It represents a small part of our budget, and we file this under community development. We do not publicize these works as they are incidental. However, they are so rewarding and meaningful to those who benefit and our donors who make them possible.

Chapter 10.
Challenging Ourselves

With this in mind, we constantly pray for you, that our God may make you worthy of his calling, and that by his power he may bring to fruition your every desire for goodness and your every deed prompted by faith.

2 Thessalonians 1:11 (NIV)

The Enemy at Work

I returned to Uganda in July 2011, accompanied by Billie, a nurse coworker and volunteer at a pregnancy resource center, and a married couple, Curtis and Rhonda, friends from church. This couple is joining us to teach an AIDS prevention program in Entebbe. I came for five weeks, having several goals to accomplish besides the Buwenge project. Our travel went well, except that Curtis carry-on luggage containing all his electronics disappeared. The flight attendant stored it away because of the lack of space in the cabin. It proved to be a great source of heartache for this couple. But with time, they overcame.

I believe this was an attack of the enemy. It usually happens when someone is stepping out in faith. Jesus said, "The thief comes only to steal and kill and destroy. I have come so that they may have life and have it to the full" (John 10:10, NIV). Satan delights in trying to thwart the purposes God has for your life. If he can discourage you or render you incapable of fulfilling the plans that God has for you, then he has succeeded. Thank God that there is a second part to that verse. Jesus helps us overcome. If we persist in our desire to serve God despite setbacks, the enemy will retreat at least for a time: "When the devil had finished all this tempting, he left him until an opportune time" (Luke 4:13, NIV).

The Rwanda Connection

Early during our stay, our team enjoyed a safari experience similar to the one I already shared and at least as memorable. I met a retired software engineer from Oakland, California. Ha, Californians, they are everywhere! His wife is a teacher; as a gift for her retirement, they enjoy safaris in several African countries: Tanzania, Kenya, Uganda, and Rwanda. This gentleman has a different focus than his wife. He is trying to come to terms with being a Holocaust survivor like his father. His visit to Rwanda is prompting him to analyze how Rwandans are dealing with their genocide compared to the Jewish people.

We talked about forgiving a *whole* people. It led us to discuss our propensity for evil, our need for forgiveness, and the necessity to forgive others no matter how undeserving. On two other occasions, we pursued our conversation and found mutual understanding. He would like to devote one month per year to helping in a developing country but does not know how. I said God would show him, and I would pray. A book such as this one can inspire and provide guidance. In the near future, we plan to provide guided opportunities to serve in Uganda.

The Doctor Comes to Visit

Dr. John (fictitious name) met us at our hotel in Kampala. He was recently assigned to the Buwenge health center 4. Dr. John lives in Jinja with his wife and their four children. I was glad to learn that he had performed abdominal surgery, including cesarean sections, in the past.

Dr. John indicated that he would be willing to stay in Buwenge and attend to the patients in difficult labor needing expert care such as cesarean sections. He noted that the doctor's house would have to be vacated and renovated. He would also like to upgrade and occupy a room next door as he needs an office.

We discussed my desire to open a pregnancy resource center either in Jinja or Kampala. He was supportive. He shared his personal experience with an unplanned pregnancy. When his daughter was seventeen, she became pregnant out of wedlock. She was a youth leader and a choir member at the church he was leading. It was very traumatic for him and his family. He reflected that he was absorbed in his many roles and failed to notice the telltale signs. With family support, his daughter graduated from high school. His granddaughter is now three years old and the joy of his life. He talks to his daughters daily and his son weekly.

I was planning for better maternal care in Buwenge, and I resolved to follow up with the improvements required at the hospital.

Fixing the Doctor's House

Billie and I went to the Buwenge hospital to assess the work needed. We met with Dr. John, Nurse Christine, and Mr. Semei. Abraham, the civil engineer, submitted his bid to fix the doctor's house and the office next door. He is asking for a whopping 14 million Ugandan shillings or $5,500. I thanked him and asked Paul for his submission. He suggested we ask Ibrahim and his crew of volunteers to paint the doctor's house. We went to visit Dr. Peter at the DHS. He assumed responsibility for the bathroom and pipework. I was delighted. This way, we would have enough funds to complete the renovation.

I always thought of ensuring adequate doctors' coverage to enable cesarean sections around the clock as needed. I asked Dr. Peter if he could reach an agreement with the private Muslim Hospital next to the Buwenge facilities. This way, doctors can take turns being on call to perform the needed surgery for both hospitals. Dr. Peter agreed to look into it. I was pleased with this possibility and felt we were getting closer to our goal.

After further discussion, Paul estimated his bid at three million ($1,200)! I was so excited. Dr. John was accommodating, "No need for drapery boxes; rods will do." We saved a lot on the painting since we had access to volunteers.

I met George, the town-council health commissioner, and said, "George, please do everything you can to keep Dr. John happy." I had good reasons to make this request. In Uganda, doctors prefer working out of their offices in the city and regional hospitals. They find better medical and diagnostic equipment in town. They also enjoy a modern lifestyle and collegial relationships.

Asad, a Gift from God

As soon as I arrived in Buwenge, Asad (a fictitious name) met me at the car and carried my bag everywhere for the next two hours. He would not leave me nor surrender the purse. Later on, as we were negotiating bids, he fell asleep on the chair, still clutching my bag. Asad and I go back to 2008, when I first started working at the hospital. He was four years old at the time. Alexis and I were distributing new clothing for the children. I recall Asad proudly wearing his golden-yellow outfit. He was among a group of children surrounding my every move. To engage them, I picked up an empty box and encouraged them to help me clean the grounds of any trash. Asad quickly grabbed the box and started carrying it around. Other kids wanted to share in this labor of love, but Asad would die on that hill: he would not surrender his duty to anyone. And so it went every time we would walk the grounds.

I often wondered why this little boy was so serious, intense, and fierce about his relationship with me. Jessica told me a little about him and his family life. Hospital workers live on hospital grounds, so everyone knows each other. Asad's parents separated a few months before I first met him. His dad, who is Muslim, brought another woman into the household, and she was pregnant. It did not work out with the first wife, so she left. Asad remained with his father, his stepmother, and the new baby. Asad went through a very traumatic separation from his mother. Is it any wonder that he was protective of his new relationship with me? I loved him so, and I still think about him often. In subsequent visits to the region, I asked about Asad, for he was not around. Someone mentioned he went to stay with his mom.

Introducing the Smart Choices Program

As soon as we arrived in Entebbe, our team joined Moses, the teacher I had met on my previous trip. Given our many emails, we discussed introducing the Smart Choices program in Uganda. In the US and under Beacon of Hope, Rhonda and Curtis teach this HIV prevention program from South Africa. This Christ-centered curriculum consists of sketches presented by young adults.

Moses shared a schedule with Rhonda and Curtis. They would teach in six schools in Entebbe and participate in a youth conference in Jinja. Moses and his team got the curriculum approved at several levels. Their work was made easier by a recent edict from President Museveni, mandating that schools teach HIV prevention. Principal Steven was scrambling to meet this requirement when Moses offered him the Smart Choices program. God was in the mix, as usual!

We met the facilitators: Emma, a social worker; Edith, a high school graduate; Fiona, a local pastor's wife; Brenda, an attorney, and George, who works with Moses. We were impressed with their qualifications.

Moses and George had planned an opening ceremony in Entebbe. Moses introduced us to Mayor Vincent, Daniel, the chief inspector for schools, program facilitators, and school teachers. We heard several speeches having in common their motto, "AIDS prevention for the good of Uganda," and expressing their welcome. Curtis did very well as he presented a synopsis of the Smart Choices program. We were surprised and touched by all the attention. The mayor was just a young man; even so, he was articulate and aware of the multiple layers of people involved. It made the newspapers before we even got started!

The Pregnancy Resource Center

Billie and I left Rhonda and Curtis in Entebbe as they would be teaching for the next four weeks. We started looking for an office for our PRC. We recalled that the best location for a PRC is close to a college or university. Therefore, we visited a students' hostel next to Makerere University in Kampala. We noticed a Marie Stopes clinic nearby. They have a reputation for encouraging abortion.

There were shops and offices on the ground floor and small lodging units on the upper levels. It seemed perfect for us. We met with Moses, the hostel custodian. We explained what the PRC was all about: our services and client target, university students. He was incredulous. Indeed these smart women could not become pregnant! I explained the failure rate of contraceptives. He was so surprised.

He shared that his daughter had graduated from the university and was working in a bank. He had not heard from her in five months, and before that, he talked to her on the phone, but she could never make herself available for a home visit, even on a holiday. He continued, "Could she be pregnant? What can I do?" I suggested he call her and express his unconditional love and support and the fact that he missed her. He absorbed this slowly. We parted soon after Moses said he would be looking for a rental for us in our price range. We prayed for him after we left.

Billie and I continued our planning. Our budget was limited; Billie reassured me that it was common for PRCs in the US to begin part-time. We considered sharing the location with another organization similarly aligned. I thought that Lubaga Hospital or the Kampala Archdiocese nearby might be possibilities. We met with staff at Lubaga Hospital and found it was not a good fit. They referred us to Dr. Sandra, the pro-life coordinator for the diocese.

Samuel, Billie, and I met with Dr. Sandra at St. Francis Hospital in Nsambya. As the pro-life coordinator for the archdiocese, she teaches respect for human life in schools and churches. Dr. Sandra showed much interest in the Smart Choices program and the Billings Ovulation Method. We talked about opening a pregnancy resource center together.

"Would that be possible?"

Dr. Sandra is already fielding calls from women and teens in distressing pregnancies. She loved the idea of a maternity home and is actively working with the diocese to secure funding. They are looking at starting a center in Lubaga. We share the same passion for pro-life work, and we are both *medical*. Dr. Sandra offered to secure an appointment with the Archdiocese of Kampala to discuss starting a PRC together.

Dr. Sandra was unable to obtain a meeting before I left the country. I spoke to the chancellor. He was reassuring: "Do not worry; it's only a question of time; the bishop is very supportive of pro-life work; maybe next time you come, it will happen."

The hotel manager was nearby and noticed my sadness. He took me by the hand and introduced me to Juliana, a former school superintendent. She listened as I voiced my disappointment. She said, "Next time you come to Uganda, I want to help you. Our hotel prides itself on our ability to get things done." She was very kind, and I felt better.

PRC and NGO Planning

I met with Samuel in Kampala and brought him up to date about the work of the alliance in Buwenge. Samuel reminded me that he was from Buwenge and was most likely born in that government hospital! He lived there with his mom, dad, and siblings until age seven; that's when his dad left his family for another woman. He lost total support from his father from then on. His mom struggled financially. He tried to find little jobs to earn enough for school fees. Later on, a US sponsor paid for his higher education.

We toured the orphanage that Samuel manages in Kampala. He did the NGO startup. The staff is attentive as they care for six babies and eleven toddlers. The place is clean and well furnished. I am pleased with this visit because it gives me confidence in Samuel as a manager.

We visited a plot of land he acquired recently just outside Kampala. Samuel offered the land to the alliance to build a PRC/maternity home. He and Edith could live on the same ground. Samuel and I always talked about the more excellent vision for our work in Uganda. Eventually, we settled on the next step, the NGO application. We were still gathering information and getting to know each other.

Samuel kept in touch during my five-week stay and accompanied me on some visits. He called me toward the end to inquire about our expenses in Uganda during this trip, covering the Buwenge Hospital, Billings Ovulation Method training, PRC/NGO including office equipment, Smart Choices program, children sponsorship, and nursing student scholarship. We spent 27,000,000 Ugandan shillings or $10,588. Samuel was pleased that our level of spending would support our NGO application. It did not take into account our travel expenses, accommodations, and ground transport. I was so thankful for God's provision and faithfulness, for Alliance supporters, for Beacon of Hope, Fr. Daniel, and WOOMB International.

As you notice, it is incredibly cost-effective to do charitable work in Uganda. In 2009, as we began our first project, I read *The Challenge for Africa*.[1] In an interview following the book's publication, Wangari

Maathai, the 2004 Nobel Prize laureate, explained the essential components necessary for the developing country to benefit from financial aid. Wangari calls them *the three legs of stability*:[2]

- Environmental-management policies

- System of democratic government

- A peaceful country

Wangari explained,

> Those legs are chiseled by a craftsman...[who] chisels all the three legs at the same time, in order to create a balance. If we don't have these three legs, no matter who comes and with whatever [loans or aid], we shall never develop.[3]

I found that Uganda meets these basic requirements. I feel safe in their country, they welcome our work, and the people cooperate with us. The government entities are competent, although I find some processes complicated, costly, and lengthy. I would like them to be streamlined.

This book and others continue to guide me as a CEO. I am personally involved in all aspects of our work as an organization and a ministry. I am accountable to God first, then to all donors as they sacrifice their precious resources to enable our work. I am also responsible to the people we are trying to help with programs that are culturally acceptable, cost-effective, proven, result-oriented, and that address the root causes of the problems.

Meeting Maria, Our Sponsored Nursing Student

I met with Maria and inquired about her nursing studies. She was doing well and loved psychiatric nursing. I wondered aloud if she would be interested in working at the PRC to counsel young ladies in crisis pregnancies. I asked her if she had any experience. Maria shared that it happened to a friend at her nursing school. Her peers were counseling her to abort. Maria encouraged her friend not to go that route. Other friends had done it, thinking that they could not let their pregnancy interfere with their schooling. Maria noted that they had dropped out of school anyway.

With her friend's knowledge, Maria met the girl's parents by herself. They were angry. Nevertheless, Maria convinced them to help their daughter return to her studies after taking the semester off. They agreed. Maria and her friend met with her parents and confirmed everything. Her friend returned to school after having her baby. Maria found the experience very rewarding. I was impressed with Maria and her level of maturity. She could be an excellent resource for our PRC.

My Ministry to Guards

After dinner, I walked the grounds at the Fairway Hotel, where I was staying for three weeks. In Uganda, sidewalks are rare. You share the narrow, unpaved, and tortuous road with *bodas*, cars, and other pedestrians while trying to avoid the ditches on both sides. The traffic is horrendous on paved roads, not a better option.

On impulse, I stopped by to meet the guard. Many businesses hire guards to protect their premises. Guards work long hours and, often, at night; they are lonely. I introduced myself to Matthis, the guard on duty.

"May I keep you company for a few minutes while you do your job?" I asked.

He acted a little surprised but quickly provided a chair. He continued to activate the barrier to let cars come in; early evening is a busy time. Matthis joined me for a few minutes as we sat outside his booth.

I asked about his working hours and commented, "It's a long shift. It must be hard at night when there is not much to do."

He nodded and added that he was glad to have a regular job. And then I continued my walk.

I met with the guard for the next three nights. I stayed ten minutes, and we talked about our work. On the fourth night, Matthis was expecting me, and he pulled out a chair. He was busy at the gate but asked me not to leave, "Please, stay longer."

I had been praying for him and wanted to share the gospel. But first, I asked him if he was scared at his job.

He said, "All the time."

I clarified, "Are you just alert and attentive or scared?"

Matthis said he was scared. He is an armed guard, as most of them are, and he carries a big rifle. Matthis must arrest the offender and call the police.

I told him, "If you are scared all the time, you are carrying too much of the burden. Jesus could help." I was thinking of the scripture,

> Come to me, all you who are weary and burdened, and I will give you rest. Take my yoke upon you and learn from me, for I am gentle and humble of heart, and you will find rest for your souls. For my yoke is easy, and my burden is light.

> Matthew 11:28–30 (NIV)

Matthis believed in Jesus, the Son of God, who died for our sins, but he had never asked Jesus to come and live in his heart. I led him in the sinner's prayer while he was letting cars come in. Matthis said, "I will do it because God sent you to talk to me every night. It never happened before." Later on, I equipped him with a brand new study Bible, which Nurse Theresa gave me last year just for that purpose. What a privilege to lead someone to Christ!

One week later, I stopped by to check on Matthis. He seemed settled and at peace. He announced he was going to visit his wife and kids in Tororo. I noticed that it was the same period when I would be teaching the Billings Ovulation Method seminar. Matthis asked where I had been for the last few days. We caught up. He said he had been reading the Christian pamphlets I gave him and his catechism. He turned down those who asked him to be involved in things he should not.

The guards' lifestyle separates them from their families. They often get together on their only day off to drink and carouse with other women. He had not seen his wife for the last several months. He was looking forward to reconnecting with her and their three kids, ages eight to fourteen. I was praying for a renewed bond between them.

Two days before leaving for the States, I met with Matthis, and he was radiant. He was back at work after visiting his wife and children. The other guard was with him, and I practiced my Luganda with them. They were delighted with my progress. Matthis had been inquiring at the hotel desk for the last two nights; the clerk said I was in but tired. I must have looked exhausted after the seminar! I think of Matthis with much affection. He remains in my heart and prayers.

Our First Teacher Training in Kampala

This long-anticipated training had finally arrived. I was excited but sober. It was my first teacher training in Uganda or anywhere else. When I announced to Marian and Marie, senior teachers at WOOMB International, that I wanted to hold a four-day training in Kampala in 2011, they invited me to Australia for a practice session. Even though I had taken the extension course preparing me to train teachers, they felt that extra preparation was necessary. I taught a whole seminar with Marie. Learning from the best, I was so thankful. Fr. Daniel from Oklahoma paid for my trip. He was also funding this training in Uganda, a blessing beyond words. Marian assigned Adelina, an experienced teacher from Australia, to share the task with me. I invited another teacher to join us, Dr. Didas from Tanzania. He traveled 1,000 miles by bus to be with us. I had not realized it was that far. I can never thank him enough.

I met with Adelina and Dr. Didas for two hours the day before to review our teaching plan and resource material. The Pope Paul VI Memorial Hotel accommodated forty-one guests. The participants began arriving at 6:30 p.m., all the way till 8:30. The traffic was so heavy at that time that we were grateful for anyone to show up at all! The attendants were nurses, doctors, priests, lay leaders, catechists, teachers, and business people. Billie, Samuel, and Edith were present. Dr. J. M., ob-gyn, and eleven nurses from Lubaga Hospital were attending. Dr. J. M. planned to start a natural family-planning clinic (NFP) at the hospital the following month.

On the first full day of training, while presenting the introduction to the Billings Ovulation Method, I shared my personal experience using hormonal contraceptives. I was a newlywed at the time, and I took the pill during the first year of our marriage. It brought several side effects that affected my relationship with my husband: mood swings, aggressive attitude, decreased libido, weight gain, and bulimia. It was a terrible start. As I shared, I cried. I had suppressed these memories for decades! It was not my plan at all to express my struggles! I got a lot of support afterward. Some said this would bring me healing; others said it would help them understand patients who complained about side effects.

The teaching progressed well. Medical people had an easier time understanding the concepts. At the end of day three, we held a session for doctors and nurses. Adelina did most of the presentation. She witnessed the development of the method in Australia as she was working with Drs. John and Evelyn Billings and other researchers. It was so exciting for participants to hear Adelina share significant discoveries. Dr. Didas had an exceptional understanding of the role of hormones in infertility. He was a great asset to our team.

Billie was having a great time, learning and meeting with so many interesting people from all walks of life. She was also excited about going home the next day. One whole month away from her family, including her precious grandchildren, was too long! Billie was an excellent companion. She was there all along to share in all aspects of our work; she offered wonderful advice regarding the PRC, her area of expertise. When we were having a victory of some kind, she would say, "God is good, so good all the time!"

The Smart Choices Program in Full Swing

Billie and I called Rhonda and Curtis to check on their progress, as they had been teaching HIV prevention for the last two weeks. The teachers were on strike! They had allowed our facilitators and students to go into the schools. There were 300 children in attendance that day. We praised God for His incredible favor.

We were all reunited for the youth conference in Jinja held in the Anglican Cathedral in the Busoga diocese. There were sixty participants, aged twenty-five to forty-five, but only a few young people, to our surprise. The Smart Choices program, developed by Doctors for Life in South Africa, encourages young people to abstain from sex before marriage, be faithful to their spouse, and do it with Christ's help.

The participants embraced the condom's message. They thought its regular use would protect them totally against pregnancy and HIV, so they were surprised to learn about their failure rate. Many participants implied that *smart choices* meant a significant shift. Even so, several signed abstinence pledges.

After the conference, the team gathered to evaluate the presentation. The first comment was, "We thought this would be a youth conference!" We agreed that God does not make mistakes. The parents who attended will be more likely to adopt the Smart Choices guidelines after viewing the videos, observing the live plays, and participating in the teaching.

Billie and I attended the last school presentation in Entebbe. There were ninety teenagers in attendance. We learned that most of those involved in advancing the program under Moses's leadership were his family members. AIDS had decimated their family. God is turning things around and using their pain to benefit others.

We were using a generator to power the computer and projector. There were cables all over the floor, some too loose to make proper connections. It can be scary at times! I engaged the children to pray as we were waiting, so they sang Christian songs. The experts resolved the technical difficulties and presented the Jesus film for kids. There were many commitments to Christ and abstinence pledges afterward. No wonder we had electrical problems! The enemy wanted to defeat us on the last day, but God did not allow him.

Besides a closing ceremony similar to the opening event we had witnessed, Moses arranged for the whole team to meet with a top government official at the Parliament in Kampala. Early evening, we met the honorable speaker of the house, Rebecca Kadaga. Moses presented a synopsis of the Smart Choices program and a written copy to Madam Speaker. He asked her to extend her support. Madam Speaker met will all individual members as cameras clicked away. It was a memorable conclusion to this multilevel effort to bring the Smart Choices program to Uganda. Teacher Moses and his family, Curtis and Ronda, and Beacon of Hope deserve our recognition and gratitude for investing their time and resources to benefit the people of Uganda. It was an incredible journey.

The Man from Rwanda

I met Jean-Marie (a fictitious name) in the business center of the Fairway Hotel. He was a Tutsi from Rwanda, the tribe that the Hutus tried to eliminate. Jean-Marie lived in Brussels and worked for the BBC as a journalist. He hosted a radio program twice a week, which aired in Burundi and Rwanda. Jean-Marie engaged callers to share their loss and their involvement with the genocide, either as victims or perpetrators. He had a thorough understanding of what led to it and was afraid it might recur if not appropriately addressed. Jean-Marie was seeking the release of four political prisoners. I kept this in prayer.

I met him again on my last day in Uganda. Jean-Marie told me the story of his survival in Rwanda during the spring of 1994. He went into captivity on five separate occasions. Each time, he thought the enemy would kill him, but every time, he escaped death. There were stories of heroism; a priest intervened several times. Jean-Marie parted suddenly, overcome with emotion.

He came back after talking to his wife and children, ages two, eight, and eleven. He had two fears: recurring genocide and fear of divorce. His marriage was good, but he worried because he was gone a lot. I prayed; even now, Jean-Marie remains in my heart.

PART 3
THE PREGNANCY
RESOURCE CENTER

Chapter 11. The Pregnancy Resource Center Is Born

Open your mouth for the speechless, in the cause of all who are appointed to die, open your mouth, judge righteously, and plead the cause of the poor and needy.

Proverbs 31:8–9 (NKJV)

Travel Difficulty Reveals the Heart

A nurse coworker joined me on this two-week trip to Uganda in February 2012. Bonnie and I would focus on opening the pregnancy resource center, spreading the knowledge of the Billings Ovulation Method, and teaching some classes at the Lubaga Hospital school of nursing in Kampala.

I met Bonnie at the airport, and we proceeded to the check-in counter. I learned that my usual baggage allowance of seventy pounds per luggage was not valid for the flight from Amsterdam to Entebbe. I had to remove twenty pounds; Bonnie was a great help. She gave clothing bags to a taxi driver who offered to drop them at the Salvation Army. She was relaxed, light-hearted, and funny. I did not know her well. It was a great comfort to realize that Bonnie was flexible from the start.

Getting off the plane after a thirty-hour journey, Bonnie and I felt dizzy. I quickly realized we must be dehydrated. We had both started taking antimalarial medication. After a good night's rest and some extra water throughout the next day, we both felt refreshed and able to carry on.

Planning Time

We made our way to Lubaga Hospital and met with Sr. Donatus, director of the nursing school. Nursing students were so excited and welcoming as we shared our desire to teach a few classes at their school. We spent the next two hours with Sr. Donatus, planning our Saturday seminar. I noted a natural family-planning clinic at the hospital; Dr. J. M. started it after attending the BOM teacher training in August 2011. I find it amazing how quickly they implement programs that meet their needs.

Dr. Daniel came to visit us at the guesthouse. He was completing his ob-gyn residency and was acting as a consultant for a new hospital project. A local NGO was starting a maternal health clinic and would like to partner with the alliance to equip the labor-and-delivery room. I agreed to meet the NGO representative to discuss this further. A few days later, I met with the director and his wife, a wonderful couple. I decided to pass on this opportunity and focus on starting the PRC.

Samuel met us at the guesthouse. He was beaming with pride when he shared that his wife was two months pregnant. After a year of marriage, they decided to use the Billings method to achieve pregnancy instead of using it to postpone it. Both ways worked beautifully for this young couple. Samuel told me it was an inspiring testimony to other couples who struggled to delay pregnancy successfully while others were trying to get pregnant.

We discussed starting the pregnancy resource center as planned. After a period of unemployment of six months, Samuel decided to accept the position of director of a child-sponsorship organization. He assured me that he would supervise the PRC and even volunteered one day per week to get it off the ground. He recommended Irene, a friend from church. She had a degree in counseling, was pro-life, and wanted to work for the alliance. Even though I was disappointed and shared my concern with Samuel, I agreed to meet Irene.

I am always concerned about *producing fruit*. After a good night's sleep, I felt better and more hopeful. During my morning study, I read the timely Word of the Lord, "I am the vine; you are the branches. If you remain in me and I in you, you will bear much fruit; apart from me, you can do nothing" (John 15:5, NIV).

I had lunch with Dr. Adolf, executive director at Lubaga Hospital.

He was of German descent and had worked in Congo and Kenya. We spoke French and enjoyed a great connection as we discussed the classes I would be teaching. He planned to attend the intro to the Billings Ovulation Method with his wife.

Bonnie and I visited a house in Bunga, off Ggaba Road, a busy area in Kampala; we passed by three universities to get there. Other NGOs occupied the space. I liked the office in the middle. The price was more than I was planning to pay but much less than on Ggaba Road.

Bonnie and Samuel discussed a project she wanted to establish in Uganda. Samuel would act as the project coordinator. It consisted of providing twelve animals to six families in Buwenge. Once animals produced offspring, community leaders would share the additional animals with other families. Interestingly, Bonnie and Samuel chose Buwenge to settle their project. God is in the business of building communities by integrating us into a meaningful whole. Bonnie returned to California and established a foundation called Wider Hearts.

We met Irene, and I offered her the job. I was impressed with her counseling skills and college preparation. Bonnie and I concluded the rental agreement while Samuel and Irene were discussing painting, furniture, and moving in. We were all in one accord; it gave me confidence because I sensed it was a God-thing.

Bonnie and I provided the nursing students training at the Lubaga Hospital school of nursing. Thirty-one participants attended the introduction to the Billings Ovulation Method. Dr. Adolf and his wife were present; he even helped me set up. After the class, they both came to the front. Dr. Adolf was beaming. He loved it, especially the science behind it. They were both delighted.

I continued teaching and offered two classes on breast-cancer prevention. The feedback was excellent, and the questions were appropriate. The nursing students just wanted more and more. Bonnie had a similar experience when she was teaching physical assessment skills.

We traveled to Jinja and settled at the Brisk Hotel Triangle on Lake Victoria. After attending a local church, Bonnie and I met with Fr. Patrick and discussed spreading the Billings Ovulation Method in the area. We agreed to hold a Billings teacher training in Jinja six months later. He asked me to contact Dorcas, the public-health nurse and Billings teacher who would coordinate that effort.

Dr. John, the Buwenge doctor, joined us for dinner at the Brisk Hotel. He had been using the newly equipped facilities for some abdominal surgeries but not cesarean sections. He was awaiting the appointment of an anesthesiologist who could live on the premises. The anesthesiologist only came when scheduled. This was not meeting the need because most cesarean sections were not planned surgeries but emergencies.

We also talked about the Billings Ovulation Method since he had a providential encounter with Dr. J. M., the ob-gyn who started an NFP clinic at Lubaga Hospital last year. Dr. J. M. talked him into supporting a Billings teacher training in Jinja. Interestingly, this is how the next seminar came to be: a combination of church and medical leadership. As advised by Fr. Patrick, I met Dorcas, and we planned the next training. It seemed everything fell into place. I am grateful to everyone that God brings into my life, even if only for a season, as we accomplish God's purposes together.

Next, Bonnie and I visited the Buwenge health center. We toured Dr. John's refurbished house. Everything came out nicely except that the new water tank was too small. We split the cost between Paul, the doctor, and the alliance; this way, everyone was happy. Dr. John was anxious to move into his new house in Buwenge.

Every hospital bed had a mosquito net and intact bedding. Soon after birth, all baby boys had planned circumcision to decrease HIV transmission. The operating room looked clean and functional. A team of three doctors was planning to perform 240 circumcisions the following week.

Our sponsored children and their mothers were doing well. Fadilah proudly said that Peace was third in her class. Padilla and little Angela came, both looking good. Joyce had one goat while Jennifer remained with three pigs. I extended the school fees as usual.

We met with Dr. Peter at the DHS. He was very supportive of the planned Billings teacher training. He had recently met with the bishop, and they had discussed family planning. He planned to inform him of the training.

I met Maria, the nursing-school student we were sponsoring. She shared her grades, and I extended the funds. I cautioned her to go to school directly to pay for her tuition, and we prayed for her safety. Bonnie and I had a steak dinner at the mall. A rare treat! We celebrated the PRC opening, although we did not need an excuse.

When we came home, I got a call from Maria. She had taken a taxi van to school as planned. Passengers filled the space like sardines. When Maria arrived, only the straps to her purse remained; the bag and the money were gone! She was devastated. Salome, a master's student from Switzerland staying at our guesthouse, shared that someone had stolen her wallet two days before. We prayed for Maria, who planned to ask the school for an extension.

I was puzzled. How could this happen when we had been praying for Maria's safety? A few minutes later, as Bonnie and I were surfing the internet, we noticed smoke in the living room. Downstairs in the kitchen, the cook had a pan on the gas-lit stove with nothing in it as the oil had burned. The flames were leaping on the sides of the pan. The young man did not see anything wrong with this; I told him to lower the flame and be cautious. His assistant, a young lady, also appeared unconcerned. I have never witnessed a similar incident afterward. What I understood was that "your enemy, the devil, prowls around like a roaring lion looking for someone to devour" (1 Peter 5:8, NIV).

Two days later, we were to leave on a safari. I woke up nauseous, dizzy, and weak; soon after, I started vomiting. Despite all my efforts to stem the tide, I had to go to the emergency room late evening at International Hospital Kampala. After a few hours of treatment, we returned home and went to sleep. I woke up feeling better, and we were able to go on our safari after all. Bonnie was ecstatic. She took tons of pictures, for every animal in the jungle made a timely appearance: antelopes, elephants, water bucks, buffaloes, gazelles, and even the king showed up!

Back in Kampala, we met the bank branch manager at the guesthouse. We opened an account for the alliance nonprofit in anticipation of becoming an NGO soon. We completed the process the next day with a deposit after assigning Samuel as a signatory. Samuel and I concluded our operational budget.

We met Dorcas, the nurse from Jinja. We discussed the next Billings Ovulation Method teacher training scheduled for August 2012. Dorcas planned to send invitations to nurses, doctors, religious leaders, and others. She anticipated this training to be very helpful to Ugandan couples; they had eight to ten children, often very close together. The Billings method would provide a worthy option to plan their families.

We left the same day for the airport. Bonnie remarked how much we had accomplished together during the preceding two weeks. We were delighted. We ended with praising God because we knew our Father was ever-present and had blessed our work.

Chapter 12. Abortion Is No Solution

Before I formed you in the womb I knew you, before you were born I set you apart; I appointed you as a prophet to the nations.

Jeremiah 1:5 (NIV)

A Visit to Buwenge

I came by myself for this two-week trip in August 2012. I write a quarterly newsletter titled LifeWatch, or a monthly *Report from Uganda*. We educate our readers on life issues and give an update about our work in Uganda. I usually invite whoever would like to join me and support the objectives of the alliance. Both are on our website, www.allianceforlifeinternational.org, under publications. I trust God to bring the right people. I want to lead groups to Uganda, but my focus has been on establishing our work there.

My first order of duty was to check on the Buwenge hospital. I met Dr. John in Kampala and gave him the equipment he requested. He was a happy man! On one of my trips to Buwenge, I shared a ride with his brother Alex, a teacher. He wanted to integrate the knowledge of God into every subject. In government schools, you learn about God only in religious classes. A level of freedom permits what Alex has in mind since 82 percent of the population is Christian. One-third of the schools are governmental; the others are confessional.

Polygamy, a Difficult Life Style

Alex just remarried recently after being separated for seven years. His wife did not share his faith, and it broke their marriage. He has three children aged nine to fourteen. He and Dr. John's father had nine wives living together and forty-one children. Thankfully, this tribal custom is on its way out. John and Alex shared the same mother. John supported eight brothers and sisters, as his father could not provide for his children.

Alex stopped by his ex-wife's house to drop matoke and a little money for the children. He prided himself in meeting his family's needs; it was his job! Alex lived in a different city with his new wife. He concluded, "We are pleased with our life, but we are not rich."

Mr. Semei received me warmly. He was almost done with his management studies and was awaiting a new assignment. I met with our sponsored children, Angela and Peace, and gave their moms, Adilla and Fadilah, their overdue monthly donations. The mothers were very encouraged.

We had opened a bank account, but the manager failed to tell us that our funds would not be accessible until the NGO was finally approved. Angela looked super. She was a healthy and bright three-year-old. While waiting for our funds, Adilla managed by renting the room we had cemented a while back. Now they occupied the main house. Her garden was thriving. Adilla asked for additional money for a mattress and bedding, goats, and a cow. The goats she had all died. I passed on for the animals but said yes to the bedroom furnishings.

Teacher Training in Jinja

I visited the facilities at Mother Generalate, a guesthouse and conference center run by the Sisters. They gave us the conference room upstairs with a balcony and views of the gardens. Our trainees will love it. I met with Dorcas, my co-teacher, and made final preparations for our seminar.

The four-day training went well. Dorcas had planned the event and invited nurses, midwives, priests, catechists, directors of nursing schools, and a representative from the Catholic Medical Bureau. I learned that the medical bureau was developing a Billings Ovulation Method curriculum for doctors in training with WOOMB International's guidance. I had only led one teacher training in Kampala, and they already had adopted the Billings method! Soon after, they made it an approved method for all Catholic medical facilities in Uganda. I found this incredibly rewarding.

Harriet and Dorcas participated in the training. Both did a great job as they shared personal experiences with teaching the Billings method in villages. Fr. Patrick taught how it could improve couples' communication. The participants loved it and asked many questions.

Abortion Is No Solution

While preparing for the training, I met a twenty-five-year-old woman at the guesthouse, doing financial audits. She inquired about our pregnancy resource center in Kampala and confided that she was eight weeks pregnant. Only her sister knew, and she was pressuring her to have an abortion. This young woman was educated and self-sufficient. I offered support and prayer. She came every day and said she felt better after we prayed. I made arrangements for a counselor to follow up. She indicated she did not plan to abort, although a miscarriage was possible.

Later on, when I checked with her, I sensed her reluctance to talk. She said she had miscarried. I met her four years later. She had a one-year-old baby and stayed with the child's father but felt that the relationship was not progressing. Often, abortion does not resolve the problem.

The French Canadian Connection

My driver Godfrey came to pick me up one day early. While waiting for me in Jinja, he met Manon, a French Canadian medical doctor who had just completed her residency in Sherbrooke, Canada. I perked up immediately because I come from Sherbrooke! My brother Jacques is also an MD and worked at the University of Sherbrooke, Faculty of Medicine and Health Sciences. For an extended part of his career, he was a professor in family medicine in charge of residents. He was gone by the time Manon did her residency.

Manon and I spoke French the whole trip up to Kampala. I taught her the Billings Ovulation Method, which she would teach to the Amerindians. I had been reading about the work of Paul Farmer, MD, in Haiti, and he was a great inspiration to me. I shared the book with

Manon, as I was hoping it would be the same for her. She was about to complete a forty-day trek in Africa as a solo traveler; I found her very brave. Godfrey and Manon got along great. They were both going through heartbreak. I believe God had been orchestrating this encounter for all of us.

During a recent flight to Uganda, I enjoyed meeting a group of French Canadians who were with Dentists without Borders. Dentistry is such a needed skill in Uganda. These were memorable encounters with the added benefit of renewing contact with French culture.

Meeting Maureen

After teaching for four days and traveling, I promised myself some rest. No such luck! Before retiring, I remembered a morning appointment at the Lubaga Hospital school of nursing. A student nurse came to the office and said she was still not feeling well. As we were waiting, I inquired about her. She showed me her medical excuse showing the last two encounters. Both were related to a severe stomach ulcer, which is often stress-related. So, I asked her what she was going through.

Maureen said her uncle was supporting her studies, and then he lost his job. The government was already paying for half of her tuition, so Maureen did not qualify for more. She was making herself sick over it. I was crying as I was praying for her. I told her I would be looking for a scholarship. She was greatly encouraged. I told Sr. Donatus, and then I stopped crying!

Teaching Student Nurses

My students were ready, all eighty-five of them. As I was working on connecting the laptop and projector, the students started singing Christian songs. I had just been telling the Lord that I did not have time for my morning devotions, and I needed His presence. The songs affected me so much that I started crying again. Besides being touched, I was tired!

During my presentation, the computer malfunctioned, and the projector became too hot to touch. Electricity went off for the rest of the teaching. I used a blackboard to teach the Billings method, and they got it. One young man said he wanted to teach it. Another nurse chimed in. I told them I would let them know about my next training.

My second teaching was about breast cancer and hormonal contraceptives. They were worried because many took Depo-Provera shots every three months. I said that usually, you needed more than one risk factor to be affected with breast cancer. I stressed that the woman at higher risk was the one who never had a first full-term pregnancy. Immature breasts were more susceptible to substances that induce cancer, such as hormonal contraceptives. On the other hand, pregnancy and breast-feeding protected the breast against cancer.

Dr. Adolf, the medical director, reviewed my presentation. Sr. Donatus commented, "He is very involved with students' training."

I visited with Rusty from the NFP clinic. She told me that many clients awaited the return to fertility after Depo-Provera. It took three to twenty-three months for ovulation to return. I gave Rusty some new teaching materials. She was so grateful!

Our Work at the Pregnancy Resource Center

I met with Irene and Krystal at the PRC. Irene was our part-time counselor. She was going on maternity leave and was training Krystal to relieve her. Irene had a counseling and Bible-study degree from Africa Renewal Christian College in Buloba; now, it is a university. Krystal had a similar degree from the same institution.

Since our opening five months prior, they had counseled nine pregnant clients. I learned a lot from them about unplanned pregnancies in Uganda. Krystal was telling me about a woman who was seven months pregnant and had just found out she was HIV positive. She was considering an abortion. The client felt in control over her unplanned pregnancy but not being HIV positive and pregnant. Krystal found a woman who experienced pregnancy in similar circumstances, and she connected them. Krystal referred the mother to HIV care for the prevention of mother-to-baby transmission.

Unplanned pregnancies among college/university students present this way: the young woman looks for a rich boyfriend in the big city.

He can be a student or an older man. By the second or third year, she is either pregnant, HIV positive, or both.

We must do a work of prevention. Irene and Krystal had been going to seven schools and churches during the previous four months, and 800 teens benefited from our program. We taught sexual-integrity education. They developed several video presentations, which I reviewed for content. I marveled at our office equipment: laptop computer, projector, printer, and phone. In the middle of Africa, I do not take anything for granted. Krystal and Irene appreciated our sophisticated work environment.

Before leaving for California, I met with Samuel. I informed him that our donations come assigned already: two donors for NFP teaching, one for a nursing scholarship, and two for children sponsorship. The rest could go to the PRC but were not yet sufficient to meet the needs of our new PRC. I told Samuel our rent was too high and we needed to negotiate a reduction, but the landlord was unavailable.

"Can you follow up, Samuel?"

He was stressed out. We discussed the salaries. Samuel said they were just right, and he did not want to reduce services. I found peace when we prayed that God would meet our needs. Back in California, I wired Samuel extra funds. My goal is always to have enough to support the PRC for the next six months. It is not always possible, but I find God is faithful.

Chapter 13. Beauty out of Ashes

To all who mourn in Israel, he will give a crown of beauty for ashes, a joyous blessing instead of mourning, festive praise instead of despair. In their righteousness, they will be like great oaks that the LORD has planted for his own glory.

Isaiah 61:3 (NLT)

Smart Choices

Back in Uganda in February 2013, I noticed two giant billboards on a busy roadway. The first one showed a young and smiling African man with the caption, "Condoms are my smart choice. I have plans for a great future." The other represented an African woman with arms folded across her chest, saying, "Implant is my smart choice. I love my career and my family."

When your competition uses your language, you may assume that they are disturbed by your message and want to cut into your business. We hope so. Smart Choices is the name of the HIV prevention program we introduced in Uganda in 2011.

I met Moses and his wife, Elizabeth, at their home in Entebbe. After introducing the program in Uganda through Beacon of Hope and the alliance, Moses and his wife Elizabeth were spreading the Smart Choices program in Kamuli and the northeast.

The Pregnancy Resource Center

My first order of business was to attend Irene's graduation from Africa Renewal Christian College. I met Jeff, the principal; he was from Ventura County in California. He conveyed his appreciation for employing Irene and Krystal, both graduates of his institution. I marveled that God connected us to His people at so many levels. We could rest in the fact that God was involved.

During this trip, I negotiated our rent and got a better deal. After our initial startup, we counseled several pregnant women. It has quieted down since. We discussed where we could publicize our services. Krystal asked for prayer. It went like this: "Oh, Dear God, thank You for providing a place where we can minister to young women distressed by their pregnancies. O Lord, prepare Krystal to become an outstanding counselor. Guide her through Your Holy Spirit. And, please, God, bring us the young women You would like us to help."

Samuel and I tried videoconferencing for the Alliance for Life International, Uganda (ALI-Uganda), board meeting. Dennis, a board member from California, was joining us. I indicated that we would have enough to cover our PRC expenses for the next five and a half months. Samuel was very pleased. Dennis was excited to meet Samuel through this new technology. Dennis brings in his vast experience as a pastor and lawyer.

I met Samuel, Edith, and Krystal at Ggaba Community Church in Kampala. Ggaba Church and Africa Renewal ministries are connected. The message was about the unity of believers. Through it, we experience God's presence, miracles, and anointing.

I was in deep thought after I learned that Dr. Evelyn Billings had just passed away. I remembered my promise to Drs. John and Evelyn Billings to bring the method to Africa. I made this promise in 2005 in Australia while attending a conference. Dr. John said, "The future of the Billings Ovulation Method belongs to Africa."

At that conference, I met a participant who taught the Billings method in Africa for twenty-five years. Soon after returning to the States, I learned that she had died suddenly. It was as if God was saying, "It's your turn." During the church service, I recommitted to spreading the knowledge of the Billings Ovulation Method in Uganda. But then, I pointed out to God my shortcomings, "I am not part of a couple like Drs. John and Evelyn." God was quick to remind me that He is my husband (Isaiah 54:5). So He is, and I go forth with a fresh anointing!

My Ministry to Guards

Back at Emmaus Guesthouse in Kampala, I talked to Bernard, a Christian security guard. He lost his parents when he was three years old. Three village women poisoned them over a feud. His Christian grandparents raised him. It was such a tragedy, but God reached out to this young boy and brought good out of this terrible situation. On his way to work every morning, he prayed with other fellow guards; a few were Christians.

During my daily walk on the grounds at Emmaus, I stopped by to talk to Ben (a fictitious name), another house guard. I went up and down the steps and all around the house. The guard's booth was on the top level. I asked Ben to join me there. I needed to recuperate; "I'm hot and tired," I said in jest. I shared the gospel with him, little by little, in between my rounds. I teased him by telling him to use this time to think about it. He accepted Christ, and I gave him my new Bible. He confided that his daughter had two abortions while attending school away from home. He felt guilty because he had forced her to abort. She had returned home and was very depressed. In the end, I prayed for him and his daughter, for healing, for forgiveness, and for beauty to spring out of ashes (based on Isaiah 61:3).

Spreading the Billings Ovulation Method

I met Irene and Krystal and taught them the Billings Method. I was not expecting them to become teachers. However, I wanted them to understand all aspects of the Alliance's work. Back at the guesthouse, I met three Billings teachers in training. All had attended the Jinja seminar. Susan was nine months pregnant. We reviewed the teaching related to breastfeeding.

Irene and I met with Regina, the health coordinator for the Archdiocese of Kampala. We discussed how to join our efforts to spread the Billings method in their healthcare facilities. We agreed to meet again on my return in six months. Irene realized how excited she was about this type of work. Her husband wanted to learn the method. It is best that both partners be involved.

The next day, I visited Lubaga Hospital in Kampala. I met Resty, in charge of public health, and the other Resty, who taught the Billings method. I continued to work with her and gave her additional teaching tools, deepened her knowledge, and encouraged her. At their nursing school, I taught a class on breast cancer and hormonal contraceptives. They had numerous questions; I found it so rewarding.

I met with Sr. Donatus, who announced her retirement. I said she was in good company since Pope Benedict and I were also retiring! We took pictures, and we prayed. We discussed Maureen's nursing scholarship. It was such a beautiful and timely visit. I am very thankful for our collaboration and friendship. Sr. Donatus was the one who invited me to teach the Billings method and related knowledge at the nursing school.

When I went to the Jinja region, I met with Dorcas, my co-teacher at the Billings teacher training in 2012. I was anxious to hear an update. My emails did not fulfill their purpose, and Dorcas apologized. Although it has improved over the years, email messages are not their preferred communication style. Dorcas indicated that our trainees enjoyed teaching the BOM. She mentioned the Buloba trainees as particularly successful with it. Ah, Buloba, it comes back in the picture!

Our Sponsored Nursing Student

While in Kampala, I met with Maria. She completed her degree as a psychiatric nurse and shared her grades: she passed the theory and distinguished herself in clinical practice. We prayed for her future career and husband.

Maria is so precious, beautiful, intelligent, humble, and sweet. She is very grateful for the help we provided. This work is proving to be most satisfying.

Visit in Buwenge

I'm staying in Jinja at Mother Generalate Guesthouse, where our Billings training took place in 2012. I can attend mass every morning. I enjoy visiting with these women of God; they are my sisters.

Jessica had joined her husband in Kumi; she was so excited about their new house! Back in Buwenge, I met Mr. Semei and became emotional over my anticipated separation from this place. He was back as an administrator and clinical officer. We visited the OR and peaked from afar as two doctors were doing circumcisions. It was being offered to boys and men as a way to prevent HIV. Cesarean sections were not yet available.

We started working with Fadilah and Adilla to promote financial independence. To supplement her income as a housekeeper, Fadilah will sell fabric, dresses, and bed sheets. Pastor David will supervise her progress. We encouraged her to start small and keep reinvesting.

We met with Angela's grandma, but Adilla was not at home. They now had five goats. Adilla planned to use the next six-month sponsorship money to buy one more goat and sell dresses. Angela looked super, a beautiful girl.

I met with Jennifer and her son Gerard. Besides the regular school fees, I gave her money to buy fruit and vegetables to sell; I did the same for Josephine and her daughter Linda.

Paul, our contractor, came to say goodbye. We visited his furniture store and his atelier. He continued to train men in construction work; women learned tailoring. There was not much crossover in terms of gender skills. The medical professions were the exception.

Back in Jinja, I met with Dr. John. He continued working in Buwenge but never used the OR for performing cesarean sections. He and other doctors were using the theatre to perform minor procedures as in the past. Why wasn't it utilized? It is hard for doctors and their families to live in villages. There were other factors. Since then, Dr. John has joined Bonnie in her work for the Wider Hearts Foundation. They conduct medical outreach in poor communities.

Since we had completed all the improvements we had agreed upon, I felt it was time to move on and work on our other goals, such as obtaining our NGO status and focusing on our pregnancy resource center.

God was faithful all along. He equipped me for the work, both through administrative skills and trusted relationships, and provided the funding. At times, I was so excited about all that we had accomplished. The Buwenge hospital project represented a wonderful first endeavor in Uganda. It gave me confidence that God would continue to guide and provide for His work. As for the use of the operating room for maternal purposes, I left this in God's hands.

Travel Encounter

On the plane from Amsterdam to the States, I met John, an environmental engineer (fictitious name, and details changed). He had been all over Africa. I like to meet professionals involved in improving the environment. I am sure we touched on the subject, but John was very interested in the work of the alliance. I think that through it, he began to trust me. It led him to share his personal life.

John was returning home to Los Angeles. His daughter was going to court to fight a manslaughter charge. She had gotten into a car accident in which her passenger died. John shared that his wife was Catholic, and he—a Methodist. He did not raise their five children in the Christian faith but instead opposed his wife. Now he regretted it. They were all young adults. I said it was not too late to reconnect with his faith and become the spiritual leader he wished to be.

As we talked about pregnancy counseling, John confided that he had an abortion experience as a young man; it was his first child. His girlfriend insisted on having an abortion even though he was willing to get married. He cried as he recounted the story. It was an exceptional encounter.

Chapter 14. This Method Is Love

Be devoted to one another in love. Honor one another above yourselves.

Romans 12:10 (NIV)

This trip in August 2013 coincided with my retirement from paid work as a case manager. I decided to stay five weeks to celebrate and get more accomplished. My goals were to offer three Billings Ovulation Method teacher trainings, present at a national pro-life conference, and train the PRC staff.

Visiting the PRC

Irene and Krystal developed ten video presentations on sexual integrity and abstinence and a hundred-page curriculum. They were on a roll!

We attended the first national pro-life conference in Namugongo, where I presented my studies on breast cancer and its relationship to abortion. I researched the subject intensely from 1996 to 2015. They loved all the stats and the science. Several picked up the fact sheets; a young seminarian named Christmas asked for a presentation copy and invited me to speak at Ggaba Seminary.

Teaching the Billings Ovulation Method in Kiryandongo

I was working with James (Jimmy), a new population officer in the Kiryandongo District. As his first action to decrease high fertility in the region, he planned to introduce the Billings method and got in touch with me through WOOMB International. He announced that we were expecting ninety participants for our first training. We had prepared for forty. Even so, I trusted God to provide. It helped when Dr. Sandra called and shared excitedly that the Uganda Episcopal Conference was introducing the Billings Ovulation Method in all their nursing schools and hospitals.

We stayed at the local parish under the gentle auspices of Fr. Thomas. Like many other parishes in Uganda, the church had been renovated, but not the classrooms or guest accommodations where Irene, Krystal, Emily, Phionah, and I stayed. It is exhausting to live in a harsh environment. Thankfully, no one allowed me to carry anything while others helped me walk on muddy and slippery paths.

Participants, ages twenty to forty-five, were mainly teachers, nurses, laypeople, and pastors. I taught the method's history and the Christian understanding of marital love, beautifully expressed in the practice of NFP. Irene observed groups during breaks. She reported that women were so excited to hear this teaching. We covered confidentiality, our privileged relationship with the couple, responsible parenthood, the abortifacient action of contraceptives, and so much more.

Irene and Krystal received an invitation to teach a pro-life message and teen abstinence education at an orphanage in Entebbe. And off they went on an exciting journey to deliver a life-saving message to Ugandan youth after working hard to develop our program.

Teaching the Billings Ovulation Method in Antal and Orussi

We moved on to Antal for our second training. Jimmy's family provided warm hospitality for several days. He assigned Mary and Consolate to assist us with our daily living activities. His sister Florence, a nun who manages a hospital in Orussi, set up our accommodations. After experiencing the previous facilities in Kiryandongo, I welcomed her help.

Thirty catechists attended our training in Antal; several did not speak English, while many joined us late. I did not expect the majority to achieve mastery of the method. Even so, the participants can promote NFP in the region. God has His purposes that He may reveal later.

I read a recent article about the local bishop who died after sustaining a cobra injury. Taking a walk with Jimmy, I asked him to bring a stick, just in case, then I commented, "It would be easy for snakes to hide in the tall grass surrounding the house. Are snakes a problem?" Jimmy was mum. The next day, I noticed a small snake coiled under my bedroom chair. I recognized the enemy at play, trying to scare me. I asked Jimmy to come and remove the intruder.

We drove to Orussi, a ninety-minute journey on rocky and winding roads, revealing a spectacular view of the valley. Sister Florence and twenty-two participants were expecting us at a small hospital. We began our training with an introduction to the method. This time, our group was more varied. Beatrice, a teacher in training, joined us.

Andrew, the clinical officer, helped the attendees during the course. Sr. Florence would start an NFP clinic, and Andrew, who already had some knowledge, would lead that effort.

Promoting the Billings Ovulation Method in Kiryandongo

Back in Kiryandongo, Jimmy and I put the final touches on our proposal to bring the Billings method to government hospitals, clinics, and other settings. As a new population officer, Jimmy was submitting his three-year work plan to address high fertility and population growth. We met with several officials to gather their support: the hospital chairman, the director of nursing, and President Museveni's representative. Jimmy met many others, but in the end, the funding did not go through.

The international community has flooded Africa with funds for artificial contraception and abortion for the last fifty years. I am glad we made that effort. Otherwise, we would have never known where to focus our energy and precious resources. Catholic healthcare welcomes the Billings method.

Chapter 15. A Real Ministry to Guards!

He said to them, "Go into all the world and preach the gospel to all creation."

Mark 16:15 (NIV)

I went by myself in August 2014 for a three-week duration. It had been one year since my last trip. When I went home in October 2013 after spending five weeks in Uganda, I quickly resettled and was anxious to enjoy my new retirement.

A Forced Detour

I intended to continue working per diem. My employer insisted I work two days per week at a minimum. I felt that this would be too much for me. It became a moot point after I was diagnosed with breast cancer in October 2013, just as I returned to the States. It showed breast cancer, stage one. Steven, Caroline, and I met with the surgeon, the oncologist, and the plastic surgeon. We decided to proceed with surgery followed by radiation. By the beginning of April 2014, I had completed the treatment to everyone's satisfaction.

I prayed intensely, seeking the Lord's will. During my last trip, Fr. Thomas from Kiryandongo said that I could get free land from the church to start a hospital. I thought it was strange that the cancer diagnosis came when I considered greater involvement in Uganda. Was this an attack from the enemy to stop me right from the start? I kept this matter in my heart, waiting for God to confirm His will. I benefited from excellent medical care during this period. It made me even more determined to offer the same to our Ugandan brothers and sisters.

Our Work at the PRC

We visited many rentals for our PRC. Our previous location was in a residential area, and our clients had difficulty reaching us. We looked at Ggaba road, which is crowded, noisy, and too expensive. We found a three-story building in Munyonyo, a top-floor unit with a front veranda overlooking Lake Victoria. Irene and Krystal chose paint colors and made arrangements to bring our office furniture to the new location. Everything was completed smoothly.

Electricity and internet had been on and off for the past three days, and I had had all kinds of computer and projector problems during the past two weeks. It made me irritable. It's time to go home! It was Sunday anyway. Why was I trying so hard to work? I went for a walk with Duane, an engineer from Pennsylvania. We joined his ministry friends, Patrick and Joan, for dinner. It was beautiful to socialize instead of working. It must be one reason why God created the Sabbath. As a nurse and throughout my career, I often worked on Sundays. Now that I am retired, I reserve Sundays for church, golf, and family, a wonderful change in my life.

Make a Joyful Noise

Living at Emmaus Guesthouse offers many opportunities to meet people from around the world. A group of music teachers from England had been staying at Emmaus for the past three weeks. During this time, they trained young orphans to play brass instruments.

I attended their concert in Nsambya at the Texas Club. It was held in a tent, with 300 in attendance and forty players aged ten to twenty. They were reading music and playing beautifully. I am not very familiar with brass instruments. I imagine they could have been playing the tuba, the euphonium, the trumpet, the bugle, the cornet, and different types of horns.

After performing several pieces of music, dancers, gymnast, and solo musicians delighted the audience even more. I must say their performance brought tears to my eyes. These young people had learned to read music and play several melodies, all in a short two weeks.

Back at Emmaus, I met Caleb, a music teacher. He was the one who would stay behind to continue the program. Caleb expected to become very homesick during the next five weeks. I encouraged him to view it one week at a time.

We parted, and I went for a walk in the neighborhood after dinner. Caleb ran behind me, all excited. He said that he had just spoken to his friend, a football star in the UK. His friend got him an interview with the BBC. Caleb now had an opportunity to share his experiences with teaching music in a Ugandan orphanage. He said he would have no problems completing his six weeks; he would work hard to show good results. I was just amazed at how God works and rejoiced to be a part of it.

Plans Fall Through

I was offering a Billings teacher training in Nebbi in the northwestern region. Sr. Florence from Orussi acted as an intermediary. I was seeking an agreement with the bishop to share the costs of the seminar. The bishop regretfully declined because the funding was not available. I offered to decrease the number of participants. Throughout this conversation, I had a poor phone connection. Our negotiation continued until the next day. Sr. Florence called back to announce that the bishop had in mind to send many people, but it should occur next year.

The God of all Comfort

Krystal called the following day and offered to come and pray with me. Samuel told her I was very disappointed over the failed negotiations for the Nebbi training. How sweet! I told Krystal I was doing better because God was helping me to accept this turn of events.

Prossy, the house manager, was wonderfully present to me. Sr. Florence called and offered support. I went to church and met Irene and Krystal.

I was sad but aware that there was something more at play. It had been one year since I retired. During that year, I went through a cancer diagnosis and treatment. It is behind me, and I am not worried about the future. Nevertheless, it was an upheaval. Since my retirement from the workplace, I felt that there were not enough people in my life. I had the same experience when I went through my divorce. In one instant, I lost thirty-five people. With retirement, I was losing another thirty people. I was adjusting, but I cried easily.

The message at church that day went like this: "My soul has an enemy, Satan. I must fight him through prayer and fasting. I must continue the work that God called me to do. I need to pray for protection for everything God gave me. Never be complacent."

With God's comfort and guidance, I am going forward; praise God.

Teacher Training in Kiruhura

We traveled to Kiruhura in southwestern Uganda with our driver, Abdul, and Phionah, my assistant teacher who comes from that area. Seith, the parish health coordinator, Phionah, and I had been planning this training for several months. After dinner, it was already dark. There was electricity in the restaurant because of a generator, but none in the parish housing. The hills and verdant valley surrounded the church. We started walking across the fields toward the housing units. Deep darkness enveloped the whole area. We only had a small penlight; even so, Seith and Phionah appeared confident. I marveled at their ability to find their way in the black of night. Just as we arrived at my cabin, the electricity came on.

We welcomed twenty-six participants, primarily nurses and midwives, including the hospital administrator. I taught the history of the Billings Ovulation Method and the Christian view of marriage. They loved that part, and it generated many questions and comments. The hospital administrator introduced himself afterward, saying he was delighted with the teaching.

Before going on with the following subject, Seith took me aside and asked if I could pay for the catering. I prepared the amount, but Seith said this was for one day only. I found the email that addressed this and showed him. He said he might have gotten this idea from a phone conversation with him while I was still in California. I recalled that the sound quality was poor. We met with the caterer and renegotiated the deal.

The attendees were alert and curious and asked pertinent questions. We were making excellent progress. Most had a medical background, and since biology and physiology are the foundations of this method, it was easier for them.

I called my driver, Abdul, to come and pick me up the next day. Seith heard me and started a discussion about Muslims. As a Christian, Seith was unsure about what relationships he should have with them. I said we should work with them and reach out to them. We do not want to marginalize them; otherwise, they can start causing problems. I shared my experience working with Muslims in Buwenge. Seith brought up the 2010 incident in Kampala, where Muslim terrorists killed many people. Seith continued, "But how do we reach out?" I suggested including them and their leaders when planning a community event. It all made sense to him, although I sensed fear. I resolved to pray.

Phionah was learning her role of assistant teacher; she was communicating effectively, although without enthusiasm. There was a relative in the audience who intimidated her. I knew this could be an issue. I should have prayed more. Phionah and Seith deserve much credit for planning the seminar, even though they had little local support. Nevertheless, we appreciated the authorization to proceed.

The group insisted on detailed introductions. For example, they wanted to know if the participants were married or not and if they were *searching*. I was the last to share on that subject. I said I had been married but was now single and that I was searching. One gentleman in the group promptly added that he was also single and searching. The whole thing was charming, and it was a first among all the sessions I have taught. At picture time, I winked at the participant who had demonstrated an interest; it was my way of saying thank-you.

Abdul, the driver, picked me up, and we got home to Kampala early in the evening. That was a good time considering the traffic in the city. I had paid Abdul the first half when he brought me to Kiruhura. I gave him the other half. Abdul said this was not the correct amount but only half. I reminded him of our agreement. Abdul insisted this was for one way only. We called his boss to negotiate, while Abdul said he could lose his job over this. His supervisor and I agreed, and I paid more money.

It was the second incident in one trip. I do not recall such misunderstandings in the past. There may be an explanation. When Godfrey was planning my trips, I focused on the bottom line. But now that I was more experienced, I sought to save money by organizing the trip myself and the myriad details. If I have guests coming with me, it is better to have an agent. I came to appreciate the fact that the Nebbi bishop postponed the seminar. If it had occurred, I would have been very short on funds.

Back at Emmaus, I delighted in a hot shower and dinner at Caffe Roma. There was no hot water at all in Kiruhura. The toilet would not flush except a couple of times; my mirror was three to three inches, and it was the planting-season aroma…Phionah commented, "Everything is easier after staying in Kiryandongo." She was right, although it had its charms.

Teaching the Billings Ovulation Method at Emmaus

For a change of pace, I taught the method to the house staff: Prossy, the manager, Winnie, the cook, Sylvia, and Justine, the kitchen help, and Rose, the housekeeper. They were all single and all searching.

What's wrong with Ugandan men? They do not want to marry. The dowry system is a substantial obstacle to family formation. The man has to pay money to the future bride's family, whatever her father demands. I witnessed an introduction or engagement at Emmaus. The man arrived with two small trucks containing: armchairs, an LG refrigerator, several cases of colas, a cow, a goat, and a rooster. I find this embarrassing, for it is essentially buying the bride. Many couples escape the system by cohabiting but not without guilt.

Suffer Little Children to Come unto Me (based on Matthew 19:14)

I went to Africa Renewal Church but did not know the service times, and I arrived forty minutes early. I sat next to the door, so I would not disrupt. Soon after, a little girl came to stay with me. She wore a pretty chiffon orange dress that complimented her beautiful brown eyes and her deep shiny skin. She just wanted to show love by touching my face, caressing my arms, and hugging me. She stayed ten minutes before she moved on. I never saw where she sat. She did not speak but only smiled.

I was looking for Samuel, Edith, Irene, or Krystal but saw no one. I only noticed George, Irene's husband; he nodded, but he was busy with video recording as usual. At the end of the second service, I spotted Krystal, and we spoke briefly. Samuel and I were supposed to hold a meeting there after church. I called him and finally connected after several attempts, and we rescheduled.

At the end of the first service, the little girl came back as if to say goodbye. There was no adult with her, just another little girl who also showed affection. They disappeared into the crowd. They were a gift from God, a touching way to welcome me into a large church far from home.

A Door of Opportunity to Spread the Billings method

I met with Emily, a Billings teacher in private practice. She attended monthly meetings at the Ministry of Health (MOH). These meetings serve to coordinate their effort in providing family planning services throughout the country. The MOH administration asked her to present a ten minutes overview of the Billings Ovulation Method. A lively period of questions and answers followed. The MOH doctors asked Emily to gather statistics to demonstrate the efficacy of the method in Uganda and its users' acceptance. Emily and I were hoping that the Lubaga Hospital NFP clinic would assist us in gathering the data.

The Billings method at Lubaga Hospital

I met with Rusty, the public health director. We discussed progress with teaching the method. Rusty said they had received a three-year grant called the Natural Plan Project to teach three natural family-planning methods. The director indicated that the NFP teachers still offered the Billings method if requested.

I visited with the other Rusty, in charge of teaching all the natural family-planning methods. We discussed gathering data, and I gave her the tool I had designed for this purpose. Rusty was already busy offering this type of support for the grant methods. I was not confident she would use it even though the information was easy to obtain.

I met Dr. Sandra and her volunteer staff at the Lubaga pro-life office nearby. I was excited to learn that she was taking the Billings-method correspondence course offered by WOOMB International. Dr. Sandra wanted to publicize the method on her weekly *Radio Maria* program. I shared with her the names of teachers and their locations. It was great collaborating with her, as we have similar goals.

A Precious Convert into the Arms of Christ

Over three days, I had been praying and sharing the gospel with Paul, a security guard at Emmaus. After coming back from dinner, Paul refused to talk to me, but I continued to pray. The following evening, as I was taking a walk on the grounds, I stopped to talk to him. He shared that he had accepted Christ in the morning after a restless night. I told him I have a ministry to guards. Paul said he knew it because the Holy Spirit would not leave him in peace until he finally surrendered. We talked about what to do as a new Christian, how to grow in Christ, etc. Praise God! It is a real ministry.

The following day, Paul invited me to spend time with him. He was luminous, and a huge smile softened his countenance. He showed gratitude and great joy over his salvation. I instructed him about finding a good Bible-believing church. I told him to expect a time of testing and the means to deal with it. I ensured he had a Bible and other Christian material. We exchanged contacts, and I prayed for God to help him grow in Christ. That is my act of surrender, a precious convert into the arms of Christ.

My Transition to Home

It is a long journey, but I always look forward to it. I reflect on the goals we have accomplished and take time to pray about everything, including my reentry. After check-in at the Entebbe airport, I receive a Delta invitation to wait in their lounge. I welcome the gift; it will make the journey easier.

On the second flight, from Amsterdam to Seattle, the airline offered first-class accommodation. I was surprised because my upgrades had always been on shorter flights. The seat becomes a bed, and the hostess equips you with a pillow, comforter, and dark eyewear. I was able to sleep very comfortably. It meant so much! The third flight to Orange County was only two hours. I arrived home refreshed. So, thank you, Delta!

Now that I am retired, I do not have to rush back to work, and I enjoy it. I resolve to plan more fun activities and be more intentional about developing non-work-related friendships. I have taken five golf lessons this summer since I live in a community where golf courses are available. I make a resolution to play at least once a week. The scripture comes to mind, "'For I know the plans I have for you,' declares the LORD, 'plans to prosper you and not to harm you, plans to give you hope and a future'" (Jeremiah 29:11, NIV). I am encouraged, and my future is bright.

Photos

A Family Affair

The rainbow, Eithne's confirmation for the hospital project

Emily and Kampala students

Mom and Nadim

Uganda, the Pearl of Africa

A historic meeting for the hospital project

A typical Kibaale family

A gift of medical books to Uganda Martyrs
University School of Medicine

Introducing health insurance in Kibaale

The gift of land

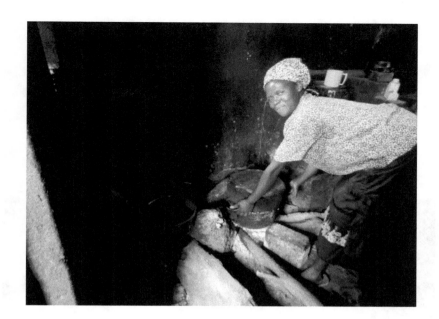

The life of Africa

The village life

Training Billings teachers

PART 4
THE ST. RAPHAEL
HOSPITAL PROJECT

Chapter 16. The Vision

Then the LORD answered me and said: "Write the vision and make it plain on tablets, that he may run who reads it. For the vision is yet for an appointed time; but at the end it will speak, and it will not lie. Though it tarries, wait for it; because it will surely come, it will not tarry."

Habakkuk 2:2–3 (NKJV)

After I recovered from my cancer diagnosis, the desire to start a hospital in Uganda came back with urgency. It required an intense period of reflection, research, and planning. In early 2015, I sought advice from my mentor Eithne. We had a friend hospitalized in Las Vegas for the past several months. Eithne and I went to visit her. The five-hour trip afforded us plenty of time to discuss the hospital project. I was curious about Eithne's reaction to the new venture. Eithne had started a nursing school in Kenya, an eight-year project that was very difficult to accomplish. Would she be in favor of building a hospital, an even more ambitious undertaking?

After much sharing and a time of prayerful reflection, Eithne committed her support to the project. The best location for the hospital pointed to midwestern Uganda. The health statistics were worse in that region. For example, I found that human medical resources were insufficient: only one doctor for 42,000 people[4] in the western area compared to one for 24,000 people elsewhere in Uganda.[5] Seventy percent of doctors practice in urban settings.[6] Doctors establish their practice in Kampala, where patients come for more sophisticated medical care. By the time they come for medical consultation in the big city, their disease has progressed to a terminal stage. The patient and the family incur many expenditures, but it is often too late to reverse course.

In 2015, I found these available health indicators: life expectancy in Uganda: fifty-nine years as the national average, only fifty-four in Western Uganda[7] while seventy-eight in the US.[8] In the midwestern region, maternal deaths are twenty-seven times greater than in the US.[9] The child-mortality rate under five years is twenty-four times higher than in the US.[10] The probability of dying between sixteen and sixty is four to five times greater in Uganda than in the UK.[11] Only four out of a hundred people attained age fifty-five years and beyond.[12] The effects of a mother's death on her remaining children: the children are ten times more likely to die early.[13]

I selected the city of Hoima, the seat of the diocese. Because prospectors had discovered oil in the region in 2006 and efforts were underway to extract it, I anticipated increased prosperity. I hoped it would facilitate the funding of a regional hospital.

How would we attract doctors to a beautiful but poor region? Being a student at heart, I imagined that the prospect of an advanced degree would entice me to move to an underserved area. Who would be offering such additional education and training for medical professionals? Since I was anticipating that the Catholic Church would provide the land and possibly partner with us, I decided to look for a Catholic university. As I was praying for a solution, I told God that a secular institution would not do, thereby erecting barriers to the project.

The Plan for a Hospital Comes Together

I was sitting at my desk in my home office in California when I did a computer search and found Uganda Martyrs University (UMU) School of Medicine in Kampala. They offered the following courses: Master of Medicine in Internal Medicine, Obstetrics and Gynecology, Pediatrics, Surgery, and Emergency Medicine. Alleluia! I formulated a plan to ask UMU to affiliate with our hospital in the western region and offer similar opportunities for doctors to become specialists.

In May 2015, as I anticipated my trip to Uganda four months later, I announced the project through Jimmy, my coworker in the Kiryandongo region since 2013. I sent Jimmy a letter explaining the project, and I asked him to help us secure a hundred acres of land for the hospital project, preferably in Hoima. Jimmy said the land could come from three sources: the government, which he represented, the king of the Bunyoro-Kitara Kingdom, or the church. I explained that this was a church project. Therefore, my preference would be for the Hoima diocese to donate land. I supported Jimmy's quest with emails and finances and planned my next trip.

Chapter 17. The St. Raphael Hospital Project Is Born

I came so that they might have life and have it more abundantly.

John 10:10b (NABRE)

In September 2015, I returned to Uganda with two guests: Sue, a Billings teacher from Canada, and Eithne. We are planning to visit the PRC in Kampala and travel to Hoima to meet the king of the Bunyoro-Kitara Kingdom. He promised us land, lots of it. We will meet partners to discuss our vision of providing modern medical care to this needy region. Afterward, we will travel to Bethesda Hospital in Soroti and conduct a Billings teacher training. If the Lord wills, we will visit the Buwenge health center 4, where it all started.

Visiting the PRC

Eithne, Sue, and I visited the PRC in Kampala. Since it opened in 2012, it was the first time we welcomed US visitors. We met with our pregnancy counselor and youth educator, a young mature Christian woman with a degree in counseling. Sue and Eithne were very impressed with her knowledge and initiative and loved our office setting. I appreciated their support.

A Historic Meeting

We were on our way to Kiryandongo to meet Jimmy, our representative, when we got a call to meet him in Hoima instead. Steven, our driver, quickly planned another route, and we found ourselves off the paved roads and into a swirl of red dust raised by numerous trucks traveling the same way.

Reaching Hoima before sunset, we met Jimmy, Godfrey, the project coordinator, and Taddeo, a land expert from the Bunyoro Kingdom. Taddeo made a land offer of forty-nine leased acres. I remarked that this was a permanent project requiring a gift of land. He was amenable to a memorandum of understanding to meet the project's needs.

Godfrey shared that the Ministry of Health (MOH) and the Ministry of Finances had recommended another location for the project. Hoima has a regional hospital and several health facilities at different planning stages. The MOH requested that we locate the hospital in the Kibaale District, a neglected area.

Eithne encouraged me when she said that I handled the lease objection well. I trust that God gives us all the guidance. I resolve to remain in faith and confident in sharing our vision for a hospital.

Land, a Precious Commodity

The following day, the six of us traveled to Kibaale to evaluate three land offers. Taddeo introduced us to the king's property, hillside landscapes with lush vegetation and endless views, as we enjoyed gentle breezes and hazy sunshine. Next, we met Cyprian, a local businessman. We toured his land and discussed his generous offer of fifty acres with a ninety-nine-year lease. The property is on the hillside and located closer to town. Our party had lunch at his guesthouse. After enjoying a delicious meal of African fare, we visited the third parcel of land, a hundred acres across the Bujuni parish, belonging to the church.

Msgr. John Mary K., the vicar general, had assembled a team to assist the project. He introduced us to Msgr. Deo Gratias, the senior priest at the parish, John, a district accountant in charge of lay ministries, Fr. Stephen, a civil engineer responsible for land and buildings, and Anatoli, an information technology businessman. Cyprian and Godfrey also belonged to this group of servant leaders.

"Which parcel of land will you settle on?" asked Msgr. Deo Gratias.

I chose the church land, and he inquired why. I said we want to be under the protection of the church, and I used an example to make my point. In 2001, I visited France and joined my brother Jacques, a medical doctor completing a sabbatical in Montpellier. He took me on a tour of the University Hospital of Montpellier, founded in 1220 and the oldest medical faculty in Europe still in operation. As we were visiting the theatre (operating room), Jacques pointed out the marble wall in front of us with the engraved names of faculty members in the 1200s, 1300s, 1400s, etc. I noticed that this 800-year-old building shared a wall with St. Peter's Cathedral. The church has linked up with institutions of higher learning for centuries. When I visited the University of Montpellier, I prayed that God would use me to influence the return of Hippocratic medicine.

The Planning Has Begun

The following day, and back in Hoima, Godfrey, Jimmy, Eithne, Sue, and I gathered for a planning meeting. Godfrey explained the way forward: he will guide us through a feasibility study, which includes many other investigations, to demonstrate that the project is needed and feasible. Msgr. Deo Gratias dropped by and encouraged us to use local construction materials and workforce. I met with Sr. Jeannette, Hoima health coordinator, and scheduled a Billings-ovulation-method teacher training for 2016.

We concluded our trip to the western region with a two-day stay at the Paraa Safari Lodge and visited Murchison Falls. The safari experience is similar to Mweya Safari Lodge at Queen Elizabeth Natural Park. Eithne and Sue reveled in it. As for me, I have gone on several safaris in Uganda. I always enjoy the experience, forever renewed and blessed.

The Young Girl at the Well

As we left the national park, we noticed a teenage girl fetching water at the well. Sue wanted to take pictures of her. We followed the girl and met her family. A few huts were arranged in a semicircle, set on a dry, dusty ground deprived of vegetation in the blistering noonday sun. Her mom held a baby who was fussy and had a runny nose. We prayed for the family, took pictures, and gave clothing while Sue slipped a bill in the mom's hands. They were so touched and appreciative. I cried and determined that we would always seek out a family to bless during all my trips.

A Sign from the Lord

We were heading east toward Soroti when we got a call from Godfrey. He announced with excitement that we were to meet the minister of finance that evening at 8 p.m. in Kibaale. Our driver, Farooq, redirected us south to Kiryandongo to pick up Jimmy, then through Masindi, Hoima, and Kibaale.

Before we reached Kibaale, we arrived at a fork in the road. Farooq branched toward the road less traveled, in a circuitous route through the mountains, on narrow, winding streets, all unpaved from Masindi. Toward the end of the afternoon, we prayed because it was not clear we would ever reach Kibaale on time. We had caught some rain along the way, always a concern on dirt roads. The next turn revealed a double rainbow with verdant hills in the valley below. Eithne exclaimed, "Here's my sign! I always ask the Lord for confirmation when I get into a new project."

As we were traveling, I realized how poor this region was. Through this sign, God seemed to confirm He would bless this venture.

Meeting the Finance Minister

We finally arrived at Starlight Hotel in Kibaale, where Godfrey had made reservations. We barely had thirty minutes before our rendezvous with Honorable Matia K. We quickly settled in our respective rooms to refresh ourselves when we learned that the minister was running late. I breathed a sigh of relief and took a shower. I was still dripping wet when Eithne knocked on my door and announced, "The minister is here!" I rushed to apply a little makeup and red lipstick. I wore an elegant dress with a black and ivory print and a flowing midi-skirt. I met Anatoli on the way; he came to ensure I would not get lost between the buildings on the way to the main lobby. I welcomed his assistance as I walked in the dark on cobblestones and high heels.

I recognized several guests milling around the lobby, all relieved by my arrival. There was Msgr. John Mary, in conversation with Godfrey, Fr. Stephen, and, I surmised, the minister; Eithne and Sue were sitting on a sofa and sipping a beverage. I smiled at everyone and walked directly toward the Honorable Minister Matia K. Being American and less formal than my hosts, I introduced myself to the minister, a gentleman in his fifties, tall and slender, and with a ready smile. I expressed my delight and gratitude for his visit as we shook hands. We talked about the project. Then I asked him what support we should expect from the government for this private, faith-based university medical center.

The minister thanked me for the project, expressed his pleasure at meeting all of us, and told us he would facilitate the project to help the economy. The teaching hospital would encourage doctors to remain in Uganda instead of studying abroad for advanced degrees.

He indicated our project would benefit from tax-exempt status for medical equipment and building material, no-cost essential drugs, and a part of doctors' salaries if our hospital serves the poor. The minister confirmed that we should meet the minister of health and the minister of education. I made a mental note that we needed to meet first with Uganda Martyrs University to establish a partnership.

I thanked Minister Matia K., Msgr. John Mary, and his appointed leaders for their support. I felt we were in good hands to move the project forward. Msgr. John Mary arranged for us ladies to eat dinner in the living room instead of going to the cafeteria, and he negotiated a 20 percent reduction for our rooms.

After everyone departed and as we were enjoying fried chicken, French fries (called "chips"), and chapati, Eithne and Sue expressed how delighted they were by all the support. Eithne talked again of the rainbow sign, and we gave God all the glory.

Sue, Eithne, and I left the following morning for Soroti, the training's location. Farooq was at the wheel; we knew we were in good hands. To our surprise, Msgr. John Mary and Godfrey were already in the parking lot to wish us safe travels. We found them incredibly supportive. We noticed that Godfrey seemed subdued and that he often looked at me. We gathered that he felt a great sense of responsibility to spearhead this project in my absence. We prayed for Godfrey and our team of servant leaders, for God to guide us through this planning season, and for His provisions. It was sobering, but I was moving in faith, with the assurance that God would meet us at every step.

Traveling in Uganda

During the journey to Soroti, we brainstormed about a name for the hospital. I asked Farooq how come his name was Farook since he was Christian. He said his real name was Christopher or Chris. A few years ago, he started working with Muslims in the driving business. They changed his name to Farook so that no one would harass him.

I asked him, "How should we call you?"

He answered, "Christopher."

At one point during the middle of the day, Christopher said, "This is not an easy ride: lots of driving. However, I am thoroughly enjoying it. I appreciate your support and flexibility."

We visited the Bethesda Hospital, a brand new thirty-bed facility with two operating rooms and modern equipment. Our hosts were connected to a southern-California congregation that helped with the financing. Next, we prepared for the training, including ordering food for thirty participants.

Eithne visited with her friends and hosts, Drs. J. and E., his wife and hospital partner. She left in the afternoon for the BOMA, where she would enjoy a little rest and recuperation before she flew back to the States the next evening. Eithne and I had an intense experience together, one that will remain indelible in our hearts and minds.

Billings Teacher Training in Soroti

Most attendees had a medical background, allowing us to move faster. Dr. J. planned to start a natural family-planning clinic at the hospital. The media secured interviews among the participants as the training progressed.

After my expose on the Christian understanding of human sexuality, Dr. E. told me she was very enlightened by it. It is easy to understand why Satan tried to oppose the doctors' plan with such determination.

Satan at Work

As soon as we arrived in Soroti, I learned through the local newspaper that a twenty-seven-year-old man had just died of electrocution; he was talking on his cell phone while it was charging. Ben had been assigned to me the first day as I set up for the training. I noticed he was using his phone in the car while charging, and the connection was touching his ear. I told him about the electrocution victim. He was aware but unconcerned.

On the first day after lunch, as I held a microphone in my hand and moved about, I kicked off my shoes because they hurt me. I suffered a terrible electric shock to my right arm. I was shaking violently and screaming while trying to drop the microphone, but my hand would not let go of it. It lasted a painful fifteen to twenty seconds. I resumed teaching without using the offending equipment; it had no lasting side effects. The whole class was visibly surprised and worried; some were laughing nervously. All were relieved when they saw me carry on till 5 p.m.

On the second day, I resolved to keep my shoes on; it was a cement floor. Could it have anything to do with it? I resumed using the microphone, although with some trepidation. This equipment had been in use for an entire year at the church. At one point, I felt I needed more light in the room. With the microphone in hand, I proceeded toward the front and pushed the metal door with my other hand. I was shocked again, but this time, it was worse. I yelled and shook and was powerless to stop it until a man ran toward me from the back of the room. He grabbed the microphone from my hand and touched the door simultaneously. He fell on the floor and broke a plastic chair into several pieces. He felt dazed but remained conscious. After a few minutes, someone helped this young man up, and he returned to his seat.

All were visibly upset, even restless, as they talked to their neighbors. They gradually settled after observing that my rescuer Robbins and I had recovered. I learned that the building must not have been grounded properly; Dr. J. commissioned the work urgently. I recalled with gratitude the Lord's promise: "Though I walk in the midst of trouble, you preserve my life" (Psalm 138:7, NIV).

Thankful Hearts

As we were leaving the area a day early, Sue and I stopped at the hospital to visit Robbins, the facility manager. He had followed Dr. J. from Northern Uganda and came to settle in Soroti to build the hospital and the church in 2013.

When we met Robbins, I asked how he was faring. He said his arm still hurts, and he is light-headed. I wondered why he ran to the front yesterday. He said he could not bear the sight a second time; he intervened and did not think of himself. I thanked him for following his heart. I said, "You may have saved my life, Robbins." I gave him the watch I had intended for the king to thank him for the land. Robbins proudly displayed a solar timepiece with a brown leather strap set in a beautiful gold case.

Visiting our First Love

We arrived at the Buwenge health center midafternoon and toured with Nurse Justine. Since the previous year, the hospital had been providing cesarean sections as needed, thereby saving lives in the process. I was finally satisfied that the DHS offered these procedures. It happened this way: as Dr. Sarah had mentioned a few years back, the government built another hospital in Buwenge. It brought doctors to the area, including specialists. When they discovered the beautiful operating room in the Buwenge health center, they used it, and their doctors included the Buwenge health center in their on-call rotation.

We visited with six-year-old Angela and her grandma. We went to the gardens, looking for Adilla, the child's mom, but we could not find her. Angela displayed a shaved head, a common practice for girls and boys in Uganda. She remained shy and serious even after giving her clothing and coloring books. Sue and I gave her grandma some financial support. Many young children surrounded her, and I suspected she cared for several of them.

A Fun Time at the Guesthouse

We went to Jinja and rented a large room at Gately on Nile. We had dinner on the patio, but we were the only guests. We enjoyed a rare treat, a steak with all the trimmings, and a bottle of red wine from South Africa. Sue and I talked about teaching the Billings Ovulation Method in our respective countries. The staff left us alone in the gardens since they had closed the restaurant. We called and called, even singing to attract someone's attention. We laughed so hard in the process. The wine had nothing to do with it! When the staff came to check on us, we ordered vanilla ice cream, the only flavor, and chocolate syrup on the side. The ice cream was coconut—my absolute favorite. Sue and I were in heaven. It was a delightful evening, a gift from God after the adventures of our trip, including the scare in Soroti. We were living the abundant life that Jesus promised to His followers. I have come to know that the greater the surrender, the more intense and meaningful are my life experiences. I found that abundant life is hidden in Christ.

Another Meeting for Our Book of Memories

Godfrey arranged a meeting with a representative from Uganda Martyrs University, Brother, Professor Francis-Xavier, an administrator at UMU. Godfrey and Cyprian were his students at one time. Because God delights in making connections, I found that Br. Francis belongs to the order of Brothers of Christian Instruction, which originated in France. He pointed out that they have a fraternity in Quebec in La Prairie. It was fun to hear him speak French.

Br. Francis asked, "Why Uganda?"

I gave him a brief history of my trips to Congo, Kenya, and Uganda. I chose Uganda because of President's Museveni pro-life stance. I felt that the government and the people would welcome our services.

Br. Francis inquired, "Why a project with the church?"

As a Christian, I explained that it made sense to me. The Christian Church has a long history of medical care and education involvement.

Anatoli took pictures and video recorded the meeting. We plan to use the photographs in a book of memories detailing our progress. Cyprian shared his vision for allied-health science schools in the long term. He discussed assigning phases to the project and stressing maternal/

child health, our specialty. We talked about the health insurance concept and how it would help finance healthcare. Cyprian convinced us that people would access care in Kibaale because they already expend much effort and costs when going to Kampala.

Cyprian is looking for a second phase in his career and has committed himself to the project. Br. Xavier-Francis added that UMUSM had graduated forty to sixty medical specialists over the last four years. He sees that affiliation is possible if we construct facilities conducive to learning.

Br. Xavier-Francis concluded this historic meeting with prayer. These men have joined us and captured our vision. Already, a bond of friendship is developing between us. We committed each other to the Lord's guidance and protection.

Sue was leaving for Entebbe; she would be flying back to Canada the next day. We went to Caffe Roma for drinks and appetizers before she left with Rhoda, my new driver in Kampala. Sue was so grateful for her trip experiences. She thanked me for the opportunity to attend the last meeting with Br. Xavier-Francis. These moments are full of significance.

The Next Step

In my Bible study this morning, I read about Solomon asking the king of Tyre to help him build the temple. Solomon writes him a great letter. The King accepts to venture with him in this new project, and they eventually become allies (1 King 5:15–26). As for me, I'm getting my guidance and help from God, who is telling me that it is time to write funding letters.

Chapter 18. Looking Back with Gratefulness

[...] always giving thanks to God the Father for everything, in the name of our Lord Jesus Christ.

Ephesians 5:20 (NIV)

Visiting the PRC

I returned to Uganda in March 2016 for a six-week duration. My
first concern was with filling out an opening at the PRC. We already
had someone providing pregnancy counseling and abstinence education on a part-time basis, so I moved her to full-time. We discussed
the clients, their needs, and how we could help them. We chose one
mother to benefit from a sponsorship under our Adopt-A-Mom program. The allowance covers her tuition and some upkeep. We chose
Patience because she lived with her mom, who volunteered to care for
her grandchild while Patience studied to become a hairstylist.

Meeting the St. Raphael Hospital Project Team

I stayed at Sunset Guesthouse, managed by Cyprian. I got settled in
a single room with an attached bathroom. It has a king-size bed with
wood posts, a mosquito net, two long narrow tables for my clothing
and other belongings, and a window with rough iron decor that pre-
vents intrusion but allows the window to be left open. It has no screen;
it is better to close the curtains at night to discourage insects from
joining me in my abode when the light is on. Electricity is on and off
but supplemented with solar power. The window opens to the gardens,
an acre of land surrounded by a tall wood fence; it is filled with palm
trees, conifers, mango, coconut, avocado trees, and multiple shrubs.

Good News for the Project

Cyprian, Anatoli, and Godfrey joined me at Sunset. I shared about a children's hospital in Mbarara, southwest Uganda, built by California donors. I contacted Lance, the project manager, and visited their church located in San Diego County. They offered to guide us in our planning process. We are welcome to visit Holy Innocents Children's Hospital in Mbarara.

Godfrey announced more good news: Msgr. John Mary would be coming to California that summer. He would visit Orange County, where Louise lived, and stay at St. Martin de Porres Church in Yorba Linda.

Cyprian led us in a beautiful prayer as he pleaded the blood of Jesus over us, ended with Our Father, an homage to Mary, and a couple of short prayers. It was a delightful mix, perfectly ecumenical.

Understanding the Needs

The next day found us at the land to pray, learn its particularities, share our enlarging vision, and discuss how to attract doctors to the region. We resolved to establish Christian facilities where the poor will also be cared for, although it cannot be entirely for free. It will be a mission hospital, allowing us to seek donations to supplement the care.

Godfrey and I gathered the information for the feasibility study while Anatoli worked on our documentary. Anatoli likes a natural look, while I prefer a more studied approach. He was videotaping ten participants in three-minute increments.

The Wisdom of God Reaches Me

Anatoli shared his wisdom with me. I paraphrased:

When something awful happens, you may view it, experience it, but do not "record it." That would leave a permanent imprint on you that you could access and "rehearse." Move on, and do not hold a grudge. Let the person go. Allow the person or business to redeem themselves.

Anatoli uses an information-technology term *record*. His teaching is biblical, "[Love] It does not envy, it does not boast, it is not proud. It is not rude, it is not self-seeking, it is not easily angered, it keeps no record of wrongs" (1 Corinthians 13:4–5, NIV; text in brackets mine).

I found an immediate application. I had requested permission to speak in churches but had not received an answer to my email. Even though I was disappointed, I decided to move on and recognize that God allows delays. The person eventually responded and explained that my email was in the junk portion. He explained how to apply and apologized for the delay.

Minister of Finance Is Calling

The Honorable Mattia K. called and invited me this evening to his house in Kibaale. Dressed in business attire, Godfrey and I met him and his delightful wife, Maria, and we chatted about our families and their upcoming trip to Washington, DC. I quickly expressed my desire to host them if they could make it to California on one of their trips. The minister asked me to sign the guest book and make sure to include my US phone number.

I gave him the latest about the hospital project and continued our discussion on public/private partnerships and their benefits for the project. He will connect us with the ministry of health to ensure a timely meeting as soon as he gets back from the US. I noted with gratitude that the roads were already under construction, as he had promised six months earlier. Minister Mattia brought up the need for a nursing school, and he recalled that Eithne, who came with me last time, had started one in Kenya.

He shared the latest life-expectancy statistic for Uganda, now at sixty-three. The average woman has six children, and most of them survive, contributing to a population explosion. Minister Mattia emphasized the need for disease prevention. We are already on board with this approach and plan to join major public health initiatives and implement them in the Kibaale region.

I later saw Minister Mattia and his wife, Maria, at the Bujuni parish, their home church in the region. Godfrey facilitated this meeting as he and the minister are family-related. I thanked God for this meaningful relationship and the opportunity to see His plan unfolds.

Field Trip to Mbarara

Our team prepared excitedly to visit the pediatric hospital in Mbarara. Having been duly introduced to the hospital management staff by their California team, we toured their facilities and sat with managers to learn about their experience.

Msgr. B. shared how the hospital came about and the growth they were experiencing. He marveled at our team: project coordinator, accountant, computer tech, medical and business expert, civil engineer, and project initiator.

"Who appointed them?" asked Msgr. B.

I informed him that Msgr. John Mary K. had assigned them at the project's inception. He knew Msgr. K. as the vicar general in the Kibaale vicariate. It was all the explanation he needed. Msgr. B. wished that business people in his community would assume some responsibilities for the hospital's management.

We observed that they were already busting at the seams; therefore, we resolved to build bigger, especially the out-patient area. A large ward hosted twelve cribs. Healthcare workers, parents, doctors, and children shared that space in a cacophony of unending sounds and activity. To imitate modern US hospitals, we prefer rooms of different sizes to accommodate one to four beds.

Their administrative manager shared that they are breaking even for the first time this year, and we learned that ninety percent of families are paying their bills. This was encouraging, a reflection of good management. We resolved to stay in touch as they extended their warm guidance and counsel as needed.

Cyprian and Fr. Stephen arranged a visit to Mbarara Regional Referral Hospital, a 600-bed government institution and teaching hospital affiliated with the medical school of Mbarara University of Science and Technology. We met with the hospital administrator, who shared freely about how to best plan for facilities designed to meet the needs of a teaching institution.

While in Kampala, the Kibaale team visited our PRC, and I conducted some business with the staff. Next, we met with Br. Francis-Xavier at a restaurant in Kampala. Anatoli interviewed him for our documentary as he explained the role that Uganda Martyrs University School of Medicine would play in training doctors.

I treated our team to pizza, salad, and colas, which we enjoyed while sitting outside in a gardenlike setting. Except for Godfrey, who traveled to Germany, the others were trying international fare for the first time. They loved the ambiance, ate cautiously, and envisioned a time when restaurants offering a variety of cuisine would open in Kibaale.

Falling into the Arms of God

As I moved out of Emmaus Guesthouse and carried a box of water bottles to the car, I experienced God's salvation. I did not see the step down, leading to the lobby. I lost my balance and was about to fall headlong on the hard tile flooring when Rio appeared, and I fell into his arms with the box of water lodged between us. I had asked Prossy, the manager, to page him because I needed help with the luggage. Here he was, reporting and asking for directions. My gratefulness to my heavenly Father knows no bounds. I transferred it to Rio, a happy beneficiary.

The First Meeting of the Hospital Project Leaders

In December 2015, I tried to hold a videoconference from my home in California, but we had poor reception. We held our first meeting in person at Sunset Guesthouse in Kibaale. Godfrey, Anatoli, John, Cyprian, Fr. Stephen, and I attended.

Godfrey reported our progress with the feasibility study, and we discussed our trip to Mbarara. The trip was a great team-building activity. As it would become customary, we concluded the meeting with prayer and blessings for the participants. Cyprian reaped immediately. He was supposed to take the bus back to Kampala early morning. A friend called and offered him a ride, leaving within the hour!

Anatoli liked our first meeting because it was *really serious*. That gave him confidence. He also commented on the Bible-reading selection I used to open the discussion. It was Nehemiah 2, which talked about rebuilding the walls of Jerusalem. We talked about the opposition that occurred and how Nehemiah dealt with it. Anatoli said, "I feel it applies to us because we are starting a big project. We are bound to be the object of scorn and ridicule by some. But the Lord will prosper us."

Teaching the Billings Ovulation Method

I planned this training with Sr. Annette, the healthcare coordinator for the Hoima diocese. Sr. Annette attracted my commiseration as she was wearing a leg cast and hopping on crutches. She injured herself while riding on her motorcycle. Here's a modern nun for you! I prayed for her recovery. Nothing is easy.

Emily was my co-teacher, but she was distracted as she prepared for a phone interview scheduled for the next day. She was focused on researching the company and was anxious about getting the job. Benjamin helped us set up the whiteboard. It was tricky and time-consuming. Emily complained of pain in her left eye; it was scratchy and reddened. We endured three hours of dusty roads to come to Hoima, so we thought it was the cause. I opened a new bottle of lubricating eye drops. Instantly, she felt better. Emily said, "When I am with you, everything is okay. God hears your prayers." I am so grateful because His provisions are sufficient.

The teacher training went well. As usual, the group particularly enjoyed the psychosocial aspect. We prayed for Emily, and everyone rejoiced when they heard that she got the job. Later on, as we were packing things after the training, Emily got a call from her motorcycle driver. He was charged with picking up her seven-year-old boy after class. After looking for him for one hour, he could not locate the child. Emily and I prayed intensely as this situation was unfolding. Later on, his sitter called to say the driver found him in the bathroom at school.

Before leaving the area, we drove by St. Andrea Kaahwa's College. Sue, who came with me in September 2015, had bought soccer balls for the students and asked for pictures. We found the school and the young people playing soccer on a Saturday morning. It was fun fulfilling her request.

Visiting a Kampala Hospital

Cyprian and I visited the China–Uganda Friendship Hospital located in Kampala and built in 2012. It is also known as the Naguru Hospital since it is on Naguru Road. China is involved in extracting the oil found in the western region. As a benefit to Uganda, they agreed to build some hospitals, including the new hospital in Buwenge.

The administrator took us on tour. The wards were small and accommodated six beds. Hundreds of patients and family members were milling around the outpatient area. I doubted they could all be seen that day because of the limited staff. I observed one employee dispensing medication, another one sitting at her desk and reading the job application section of a newspaper, and a third one talking on the phone.

The hospital provided hot cereal for breakfast; families were responsible for providing lunch and dinner according to dietary requirements. The hospital offered bed linens, but the dryer could not handle the volume. They used cords inside and outside.

In pediatrics, I met a nurse from California. We both retired from the same healthcare system. She had a child with Down syndrome and moved to Uganda with the intent to start a home for disabled children. As she was planning for this project, she worked at Naguru. She told me the hospital was only four years old, but it looked like a hundred! There was a lot of broken equipment. Diane (fictitious name) explained that instructions on the equipment came only in Chinese. Without adequate training, the staff could not operate the machines, and in their frustration, they punched all the buttons. There was no one to repair them.

Diane told me that the staff came and went as they pleased. A coworker with a bachelor's in nursing earned one million Ugandan shillings per month ($285)—a good pay. She came in at 10 a.m. and left at 2:30 p.m. She was employed full-time in the private sector and could not be late for that job. As an excuse, she offered that private-school fees are costly. Cyprian confirmed this practice. President Museveni was trying to crack down on it. He had even visited hospitals in the middle of the night to check the staffing.

Interviewing Our Future Architect

Next, Cyprian and I visited with Philip K., an architect Cyprian knew well because he built a school and daycare center in his neighborhood. As he was a specialist in contemporary architecture, his designs showed much creativity, practicality, and artistic sense. Philip had built a wide variety of buildings: hotels, hospital wings, private residences, commercial buildings, and schools. We reviewed his resume and portfolio. I was attracted to his modern designs, the style of architecture I envisioned for the hospital.

We discussed building materials that are durable, cost-efficient, and protective of the environment. Utilizing unique materials and sun studies, he has built an office building that does not require air conditioning. The roofing material will handle heavy rain and fall at an angle that should not penetrate windows. Philip recommended building reservoirs to harvest rainwater and use it to flush toilets. He will use conservative prices while using quality but not luxury building supplies.

We needed two more architect bids before making our selection. I bought the local newspaper, and in the central section, there was a three-page list of all the board-certified architects in Uganda. Our driver, Moses, commented, "God is good! What are the chances that today's paper would include this section on architects?" Philip and Envision Design Ltd. were on the list. I found two more firms willing to interview.

We met with Tom K., his firm's senior partner. Their major employer was the Ministry of Health. Tom had been designing hospitals and clinics for the past thirty-eight years but had never built a modern hospital or facility. They used cement and bricks for walls, terrazzo or cement flooring. Often, there were no private or semiprivate rooms, mostly large undivided wards.

Next, we met with Ian, a principal partner and university teacher. He had a master's in project planning and management and a PhD in urban planning. His partner Steven had worked in South Africa, where there were some modern facilities. I asked what materials we should use to build this modern hospital. They suggested burned clay, bricks, and terrazzo flooring. Working only in the Uganda healthcare system had extinguished any flame or remnant of creativity!

We asked Philip to come to Kibaale for a site survey. Our choice was easy because modern architecture in the hospital setting was almost nonexistent, and few architects had a portfolio demonstrating that expertise.

Recruiting Emily

During our time together in Hoima, I noticed that Emily was desperate to find work. She was even ready to accept a position that would take her away from her family, at least during workdays. She would hire a sitter. I wanted to hire Emily to work for the alliance as a BOM teacher, but we did not have the funds. After praying together, I proposed to WOOMB International and asked them to contribute at least part of her salary. They accepted and even went beyond my expectations. As a result, I hired Emily and opened the Billings Life Center, operated by Alliance for Life International, Uganda, and sharing the same premises. God intervened and made it possible.

God Ordered Food for Me

I went to Caffe Roma for a drink and appetizers. I ordered the beverage, but the waitress did not return to take my entire order. I was getting frustrated, but the Lord said to bear it and wait until she came on her own. I resolved to be patient. Finally, she returned with a platter of chicken and tomatoes on skewers. I said I had not ordered yet; this was not mine. She insisted I had placed that order with my drink. I accepted the plate; it looked good. Afterward, I remembered that I had said, "Please bring salt and pepper." She heard, "Chicken and skewers." God has a sense of humor. He had already ordered food for me.

Meetings at the Ministry of Health and the Ministry of Education

Besides the technicalities of starting a teaching hospital in Uganda, here are some thoughts regarding these high-level encounters. Engineer and master planner James and architect Philip joined Cyprian and me in our meeting with Dr. Timothy at the MOH. He introduced us to Dr. Speciosa, a surgeon, further educated at Harvard as a public-health expert. When she came back to Uganda, she worked for President Museveni as his vice president for ten years before joining the MOH as a consultant. Dr. Speciosa and Dr. Timothy recommended adding a specialist consultant to our team, one who had expertise in teaching hospital requirements. In a blink of an eye, she had Dr. Sam L. on the line, a university professor at a school of medicine, telling him about our team and purpose and asking him to consult with us, "giving us his highest consideration." Dr. Sam L. requested a project briefing that I quickly produced and submitted the same night.

I was negotiating a second bid with Frederick, a land surveyor that Philip recommended. Philip told him to keep the price down, "Do it for a good cause."

Next, we met with Dr. I. from the Ministry of Education. He spoke a hundred words per second but did not wait for the answers. In brief, he was concerned about the location. "Why Kibaale? How will you recruit students?"

I recognized a bias in favor of locating specialized facilities in Kampala. Dr. Sam L. offered his consultancy. Godfrey and I reviewed the guidelines we must follow to build facilities conducive to learning. The rest will wait until we construct the facilities.

In both instances, we felt God's hands guiding us. These meetings could have been intimidating, but we found favor.

Starting Health Insurance

I shared with John and Cyprian about the concept of health insurance. My previous CEO, George Halvorson, started a health insurance co-op model in Uganda in 1997 under HealthPartners, operating in the US and Uganda. I loved their co-op model and resolved to establish one in the Kibaale region. John and Cyprian will attend an information seminar to begin the process.

My Ministry to Guards is Bearing Fruit

After my walk in the Emmaus neighborhood, I stopped to talk to Ben, the guard at the guesthouse. He had been a Christian since I shared the gospel with him two years ago. Ben brought his Bible to work. He studied it when time permitted; as a result, he knew many scriptures. He told me that after he got saved, he left his girlfriend. Their relationship was not progressing. He did not meet anyone for some time, so he began praying and fasting. God brought someone who became his wife. She is a strong Christian, has a gift of encouragement, and they are expecting! He was very grateful and happy.

Looking Back with Gratefulness

It was a great conclusion to this six-week journey where we accomplished so much: we filmed a documentary, commissioned a survey and topography of the land, hired an architect and his team of engineers, visited four hospitals, consulted with the Ministry of Finance, Ministry of Health, and Ministry of Education, advanced the feasibility study, obtained a confirmation that Msgr. John Mary K. would come to California in the summer, strengthened our partnership with the church by initiating a memorandum of understanding, updated our future partner, Uganda Martyrs University, began the process of bringing health insurance to the Kibaale region, trained twenty-five new Billings teachers, hired Emily and started the Billings Life Center, and furthered the work of our pregnancy resource center.

Instead of feeling overwhelmed with these new responsibilities, I feel energized, challenged, and encouraged to move forward even though the task is much greater than our resources or human capacities. From experience, I know the Lord meets us at every turn. He leads the way and equips us as we move along. It is a journey of faith and obedience.

Chapter 19. Not Obsessing about Money Is Impossible!

> Be sure you know the conditions of your flock, give careful attention to your herds, for riches do not endure forever, and a crown is not secure for all generations.

> Proverbs 27:23–24 (NIV)

I came to Uganda in September 2016 for a whole month. My goals were to advance the St. Raphael Hospital project, equip the PRC with two computers, provide staff supervision and growth opportunities, and conduct two Billings teacher trainings.

I resolve to be a bit more relaxed about money. I am in charge of raising funds and spending them while I am accountable to the board. I keep the books, and everything has to balance. It is a heavy responsibility that I carry with great care. I consider every expense and negotiate whenever possible or find other sources. I am praying for grace in carrying this load.

I am also obsessed with my weight; I do not want to gain a pound. There are no scales around to help me keep track, and I have little control over the food and how the staff prepares it. My role model is Jesus; He was an itinerant preacher, and He was not overweight. I adopted a prayer before meals in which I ask Jesus to help me eat like Him while I remind myself that I can do all things through Christ who strengthens me (Philippians 4:13). This approach works for me, for it removes my anxiety, and my weight is stable.

St. Raphael Hospital Project

Cyprian came to visit at Emmaus Guesthouse in Kampala. He regularly travels between Kampala and Kibaale, for he has properties in both locations. Cyprian owns a medical laboratory and medical clinic in Kampala. In Kibaale, he holds and manages a guesthouse and his farm nearby. Cyprian turned fifty the day before, and for the occasion, he held a religious service in his home. He is married to Harriet, a nurse-midwife, and they have five children.

He will help set up appointments to meet with Philip, the architect, James, our engineer, and Dr. Josaphat, an ob-gyn consultant from Mulago Hospital. We will review the hospital's preliminary drawings. We are working on a feasibility study; we have to demonstrate the need for a hospital in Kibaale, and our plan has to meet all the requirements.

Cyprian updated me on the health insurance we are bringing to the Kibaale region. HealthPartners will provide a two-day seminar for twenty participants. The purpose of the training is to equip leaders in starting and managing a cooperative that will provide health insurance to groups such as schools, businesses, or membership organizations. I am so excited about making health insurance available in the region. The cost is extremely reasonable at $6.00 for a family of four for three months. Even the poor can afford these premiums; even so, it will not be easy to convince them to pay up front for the services, a new concept for Ugandans in rural areas.

Billings Ovulation Method Teacher Training in Kisoro

Since Emily joined the alliance full-time, she has helped me plan the next teacher training in Kisoro. She comes from that area. Emily prepared the venue, catering, and materials while I managed the funds, secure transportation, and developed the training schedule. St. Martin de Porres Church in Yorba Linda, CA, provided funding for the seminar.

We traveled to Kisoro with Emily and her three children, ages six to nine. They will stay with their grandmother during the training, an impromptu family vacation. We went from the central region of Kampala westbound, toward Kisoro. As we approached our destination, we admired the snow-peaked mountains, one named for each country at the confluence of Congo, Rwanda, and Uganda. We enjoyed the scenery, the verdant valleys, and the cultivated or forested mountains as we traveled on a newly constructed road, winding and revealing beautiful vistas at every turn.

Visiting a Dear Friend

Along the way, I stopped in Kabale to visit with Fr. Christmas, recently ordained and assigned at a church nearby. Emily and the kids proceeded to Kisoro. I became acquainted with Fr. Christmas when he was still a seminarian. We made it up the hills, the last few miles on unpaved roads. I pointed out to Chris, our driver, that we would find the church overlooking the city.

Several people were already on the church porch around 6 p.m., even though the prayer service was set to begin three hours later. Fr. Christmas took me on tour, and I noticed many parishioners praying inside the church. He explained that he holds a special weekend devoted to prayer; this time, their specific intention is to eradicate domestic violence.

We visited the health center located on the grounds; many churches in Uganda sponsor and manage health facilities. I met with their midwife Rose and a nurse in training. Rose would love American nurses to come and spend two weeks in her center. I took pictures and videos and shared them with a local hospital in Orange County, but no one came forward. The time will come when our work in Uganda gets more exposure—hopefully, due to this book—thereby facilitating organized trips to the region.

Working in Historic Accommodations

I made it to Kisoro for the Billings training, held at St. Gertrude Church and established in 1924; they were still using the original buildings. I was to rediscover turn-of-the-century accommodations in Africa. As anticipated, the church was accessible only after going up the hills on a rocky road made of thousands of pebbles. It was slippery and arduous even for vehicles.

The sisters living on church grounds hosted me. Sr. Elizabeth, who was young and friendly, showed me my quarters: a private bedroom furnished with a single bed, table, chair, a view of the courtyard, and the shower area down the hall. She provided a hot water basin after dinner. Sr. Elizabeth showed me how to keep the water warm for my morning ablutions. Jerry cans full of water were handy, and I was to use them to fill the toilet tank after each flushing. She added that the electricity would come on at 7 p.m. By this time, California was so far away in my mind that I adapted quickly to these circumstances.

On the eve of our seminar, Emily and I toured the parish hall facilities. Electricity was not available during the day; however, the church rented a generator. The rooms were small, dark, and dusty, furnished with old wooden desks and chairs; it was humid and musty, probably due to the dirt floors. Between each room, there were wood bars, and we managed to carefully go over without falling. We noticed the shuttered windows and hoped they would provide some fresh air when morning came. They did! Cows grazed by the windows during class. We recognized the challenges of teaching in such an environment, but we remained undeterred. It would work out because we had prayed about it, trusting God to meet our needs.

Participants trickled in, often coming from afar and using public transportation. The Ugandan people face the world with impeccable grooming and elaborate hairstyles, which women display proudly. They dress formally for most outings, presenting with freshly ironed clothing, a feat not easily accomplished because all clothes are hand-washed, dried in nature, and often pressed with an iron warmed on coals. They lack the furniture or closets to store clothing. Nothing is easy, yet they overcome with joy and serenity while maintaining the most courteous relationships with all they encounter. Ugandans are truly remarkable people.

A team of men was setting up the electricity and assembling the white-board while Emily was dusting the furniture. With an empty battery, I had difficulty restarting my computer. Emily and I had prayed for every detail, including the number of participants. She had invited forty-nine, but we only had forty packets. The room would be very crowded if everyone came. We were pleased when only thirty-nine showed up. Although we started around 10 a.m., we covered a lot of material. It took me years to relax and accept that the teaching may start later than anticipated. There are cultural traits and circumstances that are not easily reconcilable.

I wore running shoes to match the challenging terrain. Even so, Emily and Don, a trainee, walked me to the sisters' house after the training. Emily was wearing sandals as we were going downhill on the slippery rocks. She was planning to walk home one mile down the road. I said, "Absolutely not; call a taxi." She was so thankful.

Fr. Joseph invited me for tea at 4 p.m. The water was lukewarm, and the milk was cold, not the usual African tea. He was apologetic as he explained the staff had prepared it in the morning. He had been visiting sick parishioners in their homes. He was munching on pumpkin seeds as we were conversing. I became incensed about this matter, which I perceived as a lack of attention from his staff. I reminded him that he was the high priest, a senior pastor with many responsibilities, and that this was not appropriate.

Fr. Joseph had been in the parish for only two months, and he wanted to improve the conditions. He was planning a fundraising effort for the next year to build a new parish hall. The diocese had already renovated the church before he came. His mom had just arrived home after a hospital stay. He worried because she had diabetes and refused to eat. I prayed for him and his mother.

When back at the sisters' house, I enjoyed their 5 p.m. break tea, including hot water and scalding milk, chapati, pineapple, bananas, and fresh bread. I shared what Fr. Joseph had been served just one hour earlier at his residence. I asked the sisters to please investigate the matter and say something to the responsible party at the parish.

Our third and last day of BOM training went well. Thirty-six out of thirty-nine participants completed the program. We held discreet discussions on human sexuality due to men's numerous questions. Emily and I hoped to get a handful of teachers as a result of the training. Fr. Joseph came to distribute their certificates. He prayed and commissioned them to share their fertility knowledge with the local people.

Before leaving, I spoke to Don and asked him to intervene in the issue of break tea at the parish. He promised to look into it.

Emily had been without electricity for the last four days at her parents' house. She found it difficult to adapt to the rural areas now that she resided in Kampala.

I noticed that the morning mass enjoyed total attendance. By 6 a.m., several students were already singing and dancing. The poor are very close to God. He loves them so much, and they love Him back.

I found it hard to part with the sisters. We grew attached as we shared life for several days; they lived their vows of poverty before me, but they were so rich in happiness. We prayed for a new parish hall and sisters' house, and we teased each other. I remarked, and not without some concern, that Sr. Kristin ate at least twelve to fifteen bananas every day: fried bananas for breakfast, matoke at lunch and dinner, and sweet bananas for a snack. She neglected most of the other food choices available to her.

As a retort, they laughed at my outfit. It was cold in Kisoro, like wintertime, and heating was unavailable. The sisters wore ski jackets in the house. Not having such clothing available, I piled on disparate layers and looked like a hobo! We exchanged contacts as I blessed them with chocolate. Sr. Elizabeth sends me pictures and sweet wishes on her smartphone. Uganda is a strange world; the old and the new meet at every turn, surprising and delighting me in the process.

We drove back to Kampala cross-country for over twelve hours. The Kampala traffic and chaos were as bad as I had ever seen. I found myself complaining about the trucks spewing black smoke and being allowed at traffic time, over *bodas* cutting in front of vehicles without concern over their lives, and about pedestrians in the street selling their wares in this madness. The contrast between the two regions was too much for me, and I was losing my serenity until I caught myself and started praying.

Back at the PRC

My visit to the bank brought good news: we were in the process of opening a bank account for our nonprofit, a lengthy process, but we were almost there. Samuel met me at Emmaus Guesthouse afterward, and we called Dennis in the US and held a videoconference board meeting.

In my prayer time the next day, I noted that I had only ten days left before traveling back to California. I prayed fervently that our remaining work would be done timely. Then Dr. Vincent called and inquired about my progress. He was working on a second medical equipment bid and the operating budget for the St. Raphael Hospital project.

Emily followed soon afterward with a gift of colorful cotton fabric that I planned to transform into an elaborate African dress. During her visit, her husband, Nathan, called and thanked me for hiring Emily. Because of her steady income, they could now afford school fees, the primary preoccupation of all Ugandan parents. I said Emily was very well-qualified and deserved the job; he rejoined by saying, "Yes, but it's because you trained her." Working with Ugandans is very rewarding because they are smart, work hard, and are grateful for working opportunities.

I went shopping with Rhoda, my regular taxi driver and a friend. We went to Nakumatt, a large department store in Kampala. I got impatient because I could not find the simple things we needed, and I declared the outing a waste of time. Rhoda was taken aback by this criticism because these stores represented such progress. I repented and promised myself to be more careful next time.

Back in Kibaale

Anatoli and Godfrey came for a visit at Sunset Guesthouse. Anatoli and I were developing a website dedicated to the project, www.straphaelhospitalproject.com. I wrote the content, while he provided the technical expertise. Godfrey and I worked on a project proposal.

How a Deficient Healthcare System Disturbs Lives

I took a walk in the neighborhood to find out how locals perceived their healthcare system. I met with Prossy, a fifty-year-old widow living alone in Kibaale. Last year, she was diagnosed with diabetes and high blood pressure when visiting a local clinic. The doctor referred her to Mulago Hospital for care. Thankfully, her two daughters live in Kampala. A specialist prescribed medications and a diabetic regimen. Prossy lost weight and told me that she felt much better because her blood sugar and blood pressure were under control. She reported to the same doctor every six months for follow-ups.

I met Richard, a man in his forties who broke his knee three years ago. The local hospital doctor referred him to Mulago Hospital, where he saw a specialist who recommended surgery. Richard could not raise the funds needed. He lived with a disability, having limited endurance due to pain.

Next, I met with a young man in his twenties who worked as a security guard. He had suffered from back pain for the past year. The local doctor said he probably suffered an injury, but Patrick did not recall hurting himself. There were no diagnostic tools at the hospital, such as X-ray, ultrasound, or CAT scan. He lived with limitations because of the pain. For example, he could not carry water jugs.

These encounters confirmed the inadequate healthcare system in the region. Going to Kampala for care is costly and beyond the reach of most villagers. They live with chronic conditions that impair their functioning even at a young age.

The Sweet Presence of God

As I viewed the pictures I had taken so far, I came across one of Professor Vincent. Then I remembered that I had a bar of chocolate for him and was hoping I would get to see him soon. Next, someone came to the door. It was him! From Kampala!

"What brought you here?" I asked.

Vincent said, "An acquaintance passed away; I came to attend the funeral and look at my garden."

I told Vincent, "Sorry, Vincent, about the loss; I was just thinking about you!"

He said his kids would be thrilled as he received my sweet gift.

Not Obsessing About Money Is Impossible!

I noticed I was over 789,000 Ugandan shillings ($235) in my daily accounting. After investigation, I concluded that when I paid the architect, I may have used a bundle that was not intact. I thought it included five million as counted by the bank. I may have broken the pile and used some of it for expenses. I called Philip and asked him to account for the payment I sent him.

"Did I make a mistake, and by how much?"

After consideration, Philip said, "As soon as I received the payment, I paid several bills. I should have more money left over. I must be short approximately one million."

I promised to make it good when back in Kampala.

One of my goals this trip was not to obsess about money. There is no possible escape or easy way to carry out this financial responsibility. It will always be challenging. In this instance, I resolved to remove money from one bundle at a time and make it easier to identify an intact bundle.

Visiting a Local Hospital

To correctly assess the needs in the region, I visited the healthcare facilities. I met with Corinne (fictitious name), the director of nursing of the hundred-bed regional hospital in the region. We toured the mother/infant wing, buzzing with activity, as they do 400 deliveries per month. Eleven will require cesarean sections, either performed on the premises or referred out if no doctor is available to operate. The hospital has only two doctors on duty and one in training. Night staffing is challenging and accounts for most outside referrals. The Ministry of Health assigned a visiting ob-gyn consultant for three months. Dr. Sarah was upgrading the skills of the current staff to reduce the number of mothers who were dying surrounding birth.

I asked about the availability of diagnostic equipment. Corinne said they had no X-ray, ultrasound, CAT scan, or EKG; they had only one incubator for preemies. Instead, they encouraged kangaroo care; that's when the mother carries her infant skin-to-skin to simulate a continued pregnancy environment. They ran out of gloves or other supplies, thereby delaying care. They successfully treated common diseases such as malaria, diarrhea, respiratory infections, and minor injuries. Many diseases, approximately 40 percent, did not get diagnosed and treated. I enjoyed my visit with Corinne; we talked about a wide variety of subjects, a pleasant surprise for both of us.

Time to Go!

I was back in Kampala to wrap things up before flying to the States. It always comes together. People know I am here for a brief period and what I seek to accomplish. They are very dedicated to the St. Raphael Project and the PRC and seek to advance our work in any way they can.

Cyprian had arranged a meeting at Jicca Hotel in Kampala. We met with Dr. Josaphat, ob-gyn consultant, architect Philip, and Professor Vincent, business expert. We reviewed the architectural designs and how to meet the particular needs of the Ugandan population. Cyprian had catered for an elegant luncheon worthy of our guests. We are so grateful for their expertise.

I concluded my stay with a visit to the bank with Samuel. We deposited in our brand-new bank account under our NGO; it should meet the expenses for the next several months. We had an account at another bank previously, but it did not work out. This time, our church partner recommended Centenary Bank at Maperra Branch, their flagship location in Kampala, where I received excellent service over the last few weeks.

I signed on with a website hosting company to carry out our new website for the St. Raphael project. It was only partially completed, but Anatoli and I resolved to finish it while I was back home.

Then off to the airport to catch the late evening flight to Amsterdam. It is always a whirlwind of activities during each stay. I only share the most important aspects of our work and encounters for brevity's sake. It will continue at home but take another focus: financial reports, website updates, board meetings, and fundraising. The Lord carries us forward, providing the vision, the motivation, the strength, the extraordinary people He calls to serve with us, the means, and the time needed to achieve each phase. It is a blessing to serve God.

Chapter 20. I Am Working!

In his defense, Jesus said to them, "My Father is always at his work to this very day, and I too am working."

John 5:17 (NIV)

It is March 2017, and I am back in Uganda for four weeks to advance the St. Raphael Hospital project and supervise the PRC. These goals create a center of activities that occupy my life in California and Uganda, a full-time occupation, especially since I retired in 2013.

Overseeing the PRC, Our First Love

Samuel came to visit me at the guesthouse. He plans to go to Florida in ten days to attend a seminar hosted by Samaritan's Purse. Samuel is Uganda's delegate for Operation Christmas Child. Ugandans all want to come to the US. It is impressive how many realize their dreams despite the cost. Those working for NGOs or religious institutions have an advantage since it is often a functional requirement or benefit.

I gave Samuel a new laptop computer to facilitate better communication. He was granted personal and work-related use with internet time. As a nonprofit organization, our salaries are midrange. Benefits go a long way in keeping our employees happy and productive. In addition, I gave two big bags of baby clothing to the PRC. Alexis, who came to Uganda with me in 2008, is still the primary provider. The staff got a new camera, including training for its use and caution to handle it with care. St. Martin de Porres Church donated this item. I discussed goal setting as staff development is a primary objective.

Making a Home Visit

We visited a sixteen-year-old mother and her newborn baby boy. Immaculate lived with her mom and three other people in a small room. Imagine a double bed, a curtain for privacy, and a living area four by eight feet where people sit on a mat on a wood flooring and conduct most activities. The actual cooking on charcoal was done outside. Immaculate was attentive, and breastfeeding was going on well. We provided several childcare items that occasioned such gratitude and a prayer request before leaving.

Shopping for Medical Equipment

David, a representative for a medical equipment company, took me on a tour of his facilities and showed me equipment from all over the world. I met their manager and biomedical engineer. Even though it is still too early to order, we should have an idea of the cost involved. The vendor must be involved from the designing stages to ensure that we build facilities to handle such equipment as CAT scan, MRI, and radiation machines.

The Enemy Tries to Slow Me Down!

Two days after our home visit, I was feverish, nauseous, and achy. Even so, after taking some medication, I felt better. Samuel came, and we did our five-year strategic plan for the NGO recertification. At Caffe Roma for a light dinner, I had barely finished the salad when I became violently ill. An attentive server helped me clean up and even accompanied me home. I noticed insect bites on my lower legs and realized I might have malaria despite taking preventive medications. While sitting on the floor during the home visit, I recall being exposed to mosquitoes. After adequate treatment, I recovered well.

Father Agapitus, accompanied by Cyprian, came to visit and pronounced a word of prophecy, "You are on a mission of healing and consolation. You are a better Samaritan, not waiting for all to fall apart before you intervene because you want to prevent further wounding."

Father Agapitus believes the hospital project will be a catalyst for development. Their timely visit, when I felt weak and vulnerable, greatly encouraged me.

There Is a Lake Underground!

Godfrey, Msgr. Deo Gratias, and Jolley, a mechanical engineer from the Ministry of Water and Environment in Uganda, announced that our project must conduct water investigations on the ground. A facility of this size in an area where water is scarce and of poor quality must find its water source.

Jolley met me at Emmaus and shared his report. It revealed a lake underground that begins at a depth of ninety meters and is thirty meters deep. He shared his trepidation; his team's investigations did not reveal water on the first day. That evening, Jolley got on his knees and pleaded with God for guidance and wisdom. His team found water sufficient to meet all our future needs early on the second day. God has provided mightily!

Jolley wanted to visit California.

I asked, "What is of interest to you?"

He quickly answered, "Water systems!"

This man loves his job. He brings God's promise to us; we will have a great workforce (Genesis 26:14).

Our Team Workshop in Kampala

We met again at Jicca Hotel, a facility that Phillip designed and built. The hotel manager came to the car, escorted me inside, and introduced me to Richard, my helper for the day. Richard set up an easel, a projector, and a large screen and showed me the breakfast buffet next door, with waffling aromas of fried bananas, sausages, and Ugandan coffee. Anything I asked for was met with a yes and provided now. I was so proud of them; the service would not have been better in California.

I introduced the St. Raphael Hospital project and its relationship to Alliance for Life International, and Philip presented his designs. Cyprian, Dr. Josaphat B., and I evaluated the use of prefabricated materials versus permanent structures and chose the latter. Durability and permanence won over flexible accommodations and decreased costs.

The project is complex because it requires several buildings. I asked Philip to provide an integrated and unifying design. Engineer Jolley and his production engineer explained the process for water investigations, pumping and distribution system, and water recycling. Godfrey shared the feasibility study. Brother Xavier, representing Uganda Martyrs University, came to learn about the status of our project.

A few days later, the medical team met to review the designs. We discussed other health facilities on the site, such as a nursing school and housing projects for medical students, teachers, and nurses. We decided to encourage the community to provide a nursing school and housing for nurses.

The hospital project will meet the housing needs of medical residents and interns. We discussed a guesthouse to host our consultant teachers from Uganda and abroad as we encourage international exchange. We already have a vision for that house that I found in a California magazine. Dreams come true when Jesus is at the helm. We begin and conclude every meeting by giving praise and glory to God and asking for His guiding presence and provisions.

We commissioned Philip for additional drawings in a pay-as-we-go understanding. Philip shared that his computer was slow because it did not have enough RAM to accommodate all the designs. I offered the funds to upgrade and continue his work at a faster pace.

Building Our Relationship One Article at a Time

Throughout my stay, Msgr. John Mary, Bishop Vincent, our lawyer Robert, and I worked incessantly to hammer out a memorandum of understanding (MOU) between the Hoima diocese and Alliance for Life International, Uganda. Both partners desire to pursue this building project together. The MOU will capture more significant concepts of our shared vision for the teaching hospital and its operations. Dr. Sergio, Dennis, our lawyer, and board members in the US revised several drafts. We accomplished this remarkable milestone on the last day as I stopped by the lawyer's office to sign the documents.

Life in Kibaale

I have been praying for economic prosperity in the region because people must be able to afford medical care. Even though St. Raphael teaching hospital will decrease traveling expenses, there will still be costs to access care.

Taking a short walk to town, I noticed several new businesses: a grocery store, the Millennium Hotel across the street, a reupholstering shop, a building providing three business locations, loan offices, a liquor store with a pool table up front, a dress shop, a hairstylist booth, and a bus station. There were many others that I later discovered. I stopped by to pray with business owners or staff, thanking the Lord and calling on His wisdom and blessings.

Internet was not available for several hours every day, frustrating my desire to develop a social media presence or send emails. Anatoli came to the rescue, lent me a router, and showed me how to load airtime. Even so, lack of access persisted due to disturbances during the rainy season. He came back at the drop of a hat to troubleshoot computer issues and worked on our documentary.

My irritation mounted at times, and I thought about leaving the area for Kampala, where the network was better. Knowing I was being impulsive, I took a walk on the grounds at Sunset and confessed my difficulties to God. He said, "I am working!" He always acts behind the scene.

As an exercise, the Lord asked me to write down my goals for this trip. I wrote nineteen of them and noticed I had worked on them all during the past ten days, most of them unreachable without God's interventions. I decided to stay and enjoy the time off as it presented itself.

The Devil Is Back!

While taking a walk in the neighborhood after dinner, I got hit by a motorcycle coming from behind. I was walking on the left side of the road but not in the ditch. The driver yelled; I quickly moved further to the left and fell because of the impact on my lower back. I barely had a scratch on my left elbow and wrist. Dazed and worried, I checked for my purse beside me and the new camera, which appeared intact inside. An onlooker searched for my glasses and found them several feet ahead, also undamaged. The rider fell, and I asked someone to please check on him and tell him I was all right. He was greatly relieved and also uninjured. There were several witnesses; one of them I saw at church the next day when he related he had seen the accident and was surprised how well I recovered.

I expressed my gratitude to God and found comfort in the Word when I read, "Many are the troubles of the righteous, but the Lord delivers him from them all" (Psalm 34:20, NABRE).

Time to Visit the US Ambassador's Office

Spurred by my team to meet the US Ambassador to Uganda, Honorable Deborah Malec, Cyprian sought an appointment, then announced that I would meet Colette M., the deputy in charge of missions, at the US ambassador's office in Kampala. After a thirty-minute clearance process, I met Deputy Colette as she expressed regrets that the ambassador was traveling and unable to meet with me. Before joining the civil service twenty-five years ago, Colette was a hospital administrator in Orange County, California, practically in my backyard! Deputy Colette took note of ALI-Uganda's work, especially the St. Raphael Hospital project. She found my devotion to Uganda admirable and unusual.

I will change that by facilitating group travels to this beautiful country, the pearl of Africa.

Learning about Health Insurance

After attending a seminar with John in 2016, Cyprian held a two-day training for local leaders. The goal was to set up a health insurance cooperative in Kibaale and start signing up groups. The St. Luke Health Center, located in the Kibaale District, will provide healthcare for the insured. Health Partners staff provided the training, and Cyprian shared the information in Runyoro, the local language. He was very motivating and funny. Our twenty-four participants understood the significant concepts and completed an action plan. We're on our way to providing health insurance in the region. Eventually, it will enable families to access care at the future St. Raphael facilities.

God's Way

On my way to the airport with driver Moses, we got in a traffic jam. We closed the windows to restrict exhaust fumes, and it became unbearably hot in the car. I prayed because I thought I could not take it anymore.

The Lord whispered, "Call Fr. Christmas. You spoke to him the day you arrived."

I reached out to him. He had been at the dentist for a tooth extraction while having a busy Easter week. We talked about coming to the US, and we prayed together. By the time I hung up, the traffic had dissipated. God's way out for me was to turn my attention to someone in need of encouragement, not to take away my unfavorable circumstances.

Chapter 21. Our Dream Is in the Designs!

He makes everything work out according to his plan.

Ephesians 1:11 (NLT)

I'm back in Uganda in October 2017, and for four weeks; my list of goals is growing by the minute. It always seems to fit in, and we progress on all fronts. Some are intangible. We will never know the results of one-time encounters and our prayers. But we know from experience that the Lord is at work and even brief meetings matter and are part of God's plan.

The Work of the PRC

We commissioned a professional video of Sharon, a PRC client we had been helping for three years. It captured Sharon's experience with an unplanned pregnancy and how she thrived with the help of the alliance. After several takes and editing, I marveled at the result. First, the story was typical: Sharon was a second-year university student when she became pregnant. The young man bailed out because he was unable or unwilling to offer financial support. Young men do not think of themselves as good providers and do not see how they can grow into it and support the young mother in other ways. They need as much counseling as the pregnant client, but they are rarely available to receive it.

Advancing the St. Raphael Hospital Project

While in California, and since 2016, I have been sending letters of inquiry to major foundations involved in supporting international hospital capital projects. These qualifiers narrow the field considerably. Only 7 percent of funds raised for philanthropy will end up outside the US, and most will support developing markets. The majority of African nations do not fit the description. Donations to Uganda in the health sector are for small projects such as improving nutrition or maternal and child health. As a project coordinator, Godfrey is also aware of international funding sources. We work together to identify them and send letters or proposals.

I met with David, the medical equipment representative, and I requested another proposal to provide other sources for equipment. The first included sources such as China, Turkey, and India. We shall evaluate equipment from Israel, Germany, the US, Japan, or other developed countries. David is familiar with hospital designs, and he offered to help with our review.

Designs Review, Where Dreams Come True

David, Cyprian, two obstetric nurses, and I joined Philip to review his drawings. While the nurses and Cyprian focused on the ob-gyn, labor-and-delivery room, nursery, and neonatal ICU, David and I worked on the pediatric designs. Philip later implemented our recommendations.

We held one more session with David and his coworker Shalinder and Etienne, a hospital administrator. With his vast experience in hospital management, Etienne also helped me develop our mission, vision, and core values.

While working on the designs, mechanics were repairing David's car. It was 5 p.m. when David said he would leave when his vehicle was ready. I quipped that since I needed him for an extra hour, I was praying that his car would not be ready until then. As we walked to his car at 6 p.m., the mechanics had just finished. We laughed and marveled that God was on my side.

Growing our Partnership with Uganda Martyrs University

Br. Francis-Xavier arranged a meeting with Vice Chancellor John M. from UMU. Cyprian and Godfrey joined us for lunch at Cafe Javas, a California-style restaurant in Kampala. After a project briefing, we displayed the drawings spread on adjacent tables. They loved them!

Vice Chancellor M. found our executive-style golf-course idea most innovative and attractive. He said he was arranging a meeting between the medical doctors and professors who would be involved in developing the teaching component for the St. Raphael training hospital.

Vice Chancellor M. is a mature Christian. We share the same ethical values, strengthening our passion for practicing Hippocratic medicine in Uganda. Our team, composed of John, Cyprian, Godfrey, Anatoli, and Fr. Stephen, met with Professor Michael, in charge of academic affairs at UMU, and several doctors/professors from their school of medicine at Nsambya Hospital in Kampala. After introducing the project, we looked at the designs, answered questions, and discussed the way forward. They were enthusiastic about the hospital and its role in training doctors in four specialty areas. They recommended we build a guesthouse to accommodate visiting doctors who would teach at St. Raphael.

A global health expert advised us to work with other organizations and provide nutritional or other programs. She said it would help the sustainability of the project. We learned that the Uganda Medical Bureau would also contribute operational funding to supplement the government's participation in public/private partnerships. It was a great meeting because they loved the project and were excited to work with us.

Teaching the Billings Ovulation Method in Kibaale

Sr. Maria from the St. Luke Health Center at the Bujuni parish helped prepare a teacher training at Sunset Guesthouse. Fourteen healthcare workers came from all over western and northern Uganda. Emily and I had delightful encounters with the nuns from Moyo as we discussed the method, contraception, and human sexuality. They suggested we conduct an educational TV program. They were excited to hear about our plans to start a radio outreach instead.

I was stressed because most participants had not arrived by 9:30 a.m. I forgot to leave the first hour for registration and breakfast. I consulted with Maria and Emily, and we prayed. I calmed down when I decided to go with the flow! We started with breakfast and concluded the day at 5 p.m. instead of 4:30 p.m. Usually, the electricity was sporadic, so we prayed about it. We coordinated our use of computer video presentations with the availability of electricity, back and forth all day. God gave us just the power we needed when we needed it. We serve an economic God!

Sr. Maria worked very hard to recruit, confirm, and make accommodation arrangements for several attendees. She wanted to complete a bachelor's in healthcare administration, but the available weekend programs were several hours away. We wished there would be a better way, such as an online curriculum. Current programs are so far beyond what anyone could afford in Uganda. When I met with Ms. Catherine, the commissioner of nursing at the Ministry of Health, and Emily, in charge of reproductive health, they inquired what our St. Raphael teaching hospital would offer nurses. Catherine wanted nursing specialty programs at the master's level; they would provide opportunities for nurses to gain extra responsibility, pay, and recognition. I promised to stay in touch with my nursing colleagues.

A Little Rest and Recreation

When I travel by myself and for a short duration, I rarely plan social activities unless related to work. I want to make every minute count. When guests come with me, we enjoy touristic activities such as safaris, cultural dances, historical areas, the source of the Nile, waterfalls, and shopping for cultural artifacts.

But this Sunday was different. Vincent, the business consultant for the hospital project, and his wife, Juliet, invited me for lunch at their home in Namugongo. I met their children, Justin and Jerome, as we enjoyed delicious African fare. We visited Sr. Florence from Orussi Hospital; she was staying with family as she was recovering from an illness.

We enjoyed cultural dances and African music at the Nature Cultural Center in Ntinda. What outstanding performances; they required such incredible stamina. I had a wonderful time with my friends.

Praying for the Sick

At Christian Glory House in Kampala, Deus stopped by. He was a new pastor attending a two-week seminar. He had a severe tooth-ache two days prior and ran out of acetaminophen. So, I gave him the same but extra-strength tablets. The medication made a difference and allowed him to sleep well for the first time since the pain began. As usual, I offered to pray. He immediately knelt before me. What a humble and sweet man. My efforts were meager compared to our Lord's mighty power.

Chapter 22. The Trip of a Lifetime

> Now to him who is able to do immeasurably more than all we ask or imagine according to his power that is at work within us.

> Ephesians 3:20 (NIV)

In 2017, a group representing WOOMB International at the Commission on the Status of Women (CSW) asked me to be one of the presenters. I have belonged to this group since 2010, and I have represented WOOMB International several times since then. The US embassy initially denied Emily's visa. Having a contact at the US embassy in Uganda, I asked for intervention on her behalf. Someone tactfully confirmed that Emily would attend the CSW in New York, a prestigious UN conference and that ALI-UG, an established NGO in Uganda, was sponsoring Emily. Her visa was granted one week before travel. I had bought plane tickets and made hotel reservations as if Emily were coming. I learned this principle early: pray and take the actions necessary to bring about the desired results and trust God to do the rest.

I arrived before Emily and met her at the airport. It was snowing, windy, and cold in New York City, but nothing could dampen our joy and excitement. We stayed in the middle of Times Square at the Washington Jefferson Hotel, close to the theatre district, Rockefeller Center, and St. Patrick's Cathedral.

We attended a parallel event at the Church Center of the United Nations. We joined a WOOMB International caucus where Emily and I and two others would be presenting. Our slide presentation was entitled "Using the Billings Ovulation Method Leads to Better Health and Productivity." Several attendees stopped to meet us afterward and shared that our teaching encouraged them to remain chaste before marriage and adopt natural family planning when the time comes. Our data was very positive and exciting to them.

We celebrated at C'est la Vie, a French restaurant across from our hotel. Anne joined us, a fellow Canadian and BOM teacher. On Sunday, Emily and I attended Times Square Church, an interdenominational congregation representing several nations. It was located in a theatre, as evidenced by the ornate gilded decor and red velvet seats. The music, singing, and preaching filled us with awe, joy, and hope as we imagined heaven would surpass the grandeur we were experiencing.

We were anticipating another exciting and incredible event. Emily and I expected her husband to join us in New York City for three nights. Nathan is an NGO director in Uganda. He would be presenting at a conference in Washington, DC, in a few days. He would hop on a train and join us in New York at the UN. I was concerned he may not be allowed because of the pass system. Not to worry—Nathan had broad access.

As we were attending sessions at the UN, we received word that Nathan was in the building. I stayed in the main lobby in case he would come there first while Emily went trolling the halls. They appeared twenty minutes later, smiling and holding hands. I promised them one night by themselves at a hotel. The Washington Jefferson Hotel was full, so I found a computer nearby and searched for an affordable hotel room. After drinks and appetizers, they took the train to their home for the night. Emily was scared to wander in NYC, but Nathan showed himself as an expert traveler.

Both joined me at the Salvation Army auditorium for our scheduled presentation, a parallel event in conjunction with the UN CSW conference. It started snowing heavily during the night, and by late morning, it had become a blizzard. Airports closed down, and the streets were empty. A few brave souls attended our conference early morning.

Allyson and Monica, WOOMB representatives from the US and Canada, organized this event titled Empowering Rural Women and

Girls with the Billings Ovulation Method. Allyson had assembled a dozen participants from all over the US to share their experiences using the Billings method. She was using the computer technology we are all familiar with now, but it was in its infancy in 2018 and required a great deal of skill, determination, and God's blessings for it to work. It captured all the participants on video and in real time. Monica acted as the event coordinator. Emily and I shared our research using a slide presentation. Then, Nathan and Emily gave their testimony and how following this method helped their relationship.

This experience cemented our friendship for years to come. The hand of God was present throughout to enable Emily and Nathan to take the trip of a lifetime together while sharing their intimate knowledge of the method.

Chapter 23. God at the Center

He is before all things, and in him all things hold together.

Colossians 1:17 (NIV)

Back in Uganda in April 2018, I prepared for a four-week program of activities to advance the St. Raphael project and the work of the PRC, offer Billings teacher training, and promote health insurance in the Kibaale region.

Supporting the PRC

I always rejoice when meeting with the staff. First, the fun part, shower them with baby clothing, daily planners, pens and notebooks, and gifts! Every child's outfit helps the new mother connect with her baby and realize that God is already providing for their needs. I bring makeup and small bottles of famous perfumes, and they divide the bounty. I follow with improving their skills, this time by teaching about intimate partner violence. Then I do financial accountability and plan the next Billings training with Emily.

Out of the Struggle

I read the newspaper to get the latest news. President Museveni is struggling with medical doctors. They have been on strike for weeks in order to get better pay, well-equipped hospitals, and specialization opportunities in Uganda. President Museveni announced he is hiring 200 Cuban doctors to address the shortage of medical doctors in several regions. He complained that doctors only want to work in big population centers such as Kampala, thereby neglecting rural areas where most Ugandans live. I can empathize with both sides. I pray that the struggle will improve patient access to good medical care outside Kampala.

Life Matters Radio Outreach

An opportunity to have our radio program presented itself six months prior, when Emily and I attended an event sponsored by the radio station. After writing the concept for the program, we signed the contract and went on the air! We are on familyradio.com, 103.5 FM, a Christian radio station based in Kitintale, a Kampala suburb, with a powerful reach within a 150 miles radius.

God at the Center

When meeting with Philip, he expressed his dissatisfaction with the chapel's location. After several considerations, and as I was looking at the very center of the medical complex, I found a space between the buildings designated as a garden. First, we considered a cafeteria, but we both realized we could enclose this space to host a two-story chapel in a triangular structure. Philip loved it, quickly went to work, and said, "Now I can submit my designs to the bishop!"

Pursuing a Trail

Before leaving for Uganda, I met Brenda (a fictitious name) through an acquaintance; she knew a potential donor for the hospital project. I had not sent a letter to his foundation, but I found many reasons why I should. This person was very wealthy, had founded a private institution, was pro-life, and was a strong Christian. I had attended an event where he was the main speaker and had read his autobiography. I felt I knew the man!

Brenda said she would contact him, having worked with him in the past. I prepared a letter of inquiry, followed by a proposal and designs. Brenda rarely answered her emails and was better reached through phone calls. Her life was in turmoil, and I felt guilty even asking her to follow up on her offer. I prayed for Brenda regardless of her ability to help in setting up meetings with the foundation. I was hoping against hope for too long.

I sought anxiety relief in prayer and God's Word. With time, I compared my situation to Joseph, son of Jacob (Genesis 40 and 41). While in prison, he helped a prisoner, the king's cupbearer, prove his innocence, resulting in his release from prison. Joseph asked the cupbearer to say a good word on his behalf to the king. However, two years elapsed until the cupbearer remembered this conversation with Joseph.

I could identify with Joseph, waiting anxiously for an answer until I realized I had trusted the wrong person. The Lord will provide for the hospital project using the paths He chooses.

As you are reading this book, is God touching your heart? It may be that God is calling you to support the St. Raphael Hospital project and become a founding member.

Offering Health Insurance

During my previous stay, we planned for our insurance team to visit other cooperatives located in Mbarara and the surrounding region. Any opportunity for travel is exciting. On their return, Cyprian and the co-op board started the business. Let's say a farmers' organization meets monthly. If 60 percent of their members agree to obtain health insurance through the cooperative, they and their household can become insured. Under Sr. Maria's leadership, St. Luke Healthcare Center provides care for the insured.

We hired Amelia, a HealthPartners trainer, to set up our office at St. Luke, sign up groups and schools, and train a health insurance coordinator. We knew we could not afford her in the long term, but we were so grateful for her willingness to stay in Kibaale for five months. Her salary and accommodations came from three sources: St. Luke, the alliance, and Sunset Guesthouse, an excellent collaboration that is a reflection of God's providence.

Getting Unstuck

The St. Raphael team traveled to Kampala for a meeting with the architect. To our surprise, four civil engineers joined us; I was expecting one. They did not push their agenda at that time but determined that our project was not making significant progress and was likely to die on the vine. Their questions generated a lot of discussions and shook things up. We needed more detailed drawings and a deadline for the feasibility study. When Philip said he would reassign staff, I provided extra financial support. Philip said he would buy a new computer. He was excited and equipped for the increased demands.

I visited construction sites with engineer Hermon and learned about making cement blocks. It may be helpful for us on our land since Kibaale has many rock formations.

Meeting our Partner

Having made progress with the St. Raphael project, Godfrey, Philip, and I met with Vice Chancellor John M. at Cafe Javas. We showed him the last preliminary drawings, including a 3D rendition. Anatoli, our IT, prompted us to discuss the computer room placement as it takes a spacious area. We are also planning a radio station in that location. Vice Chancellor M. was impressed with the designs and indicated it was time to develop an MOU between partners.

Teacher Training in Kibaale

Sr. Maria set up another training in the region, focusing on nurses, midwives, and teachers working in the private Christian sector. We found them more receptive to natural family planning methods.

Emily and I addressed twenty-five participants who were eager to learn and apply their knowledge, first for themselves. The Billings found that understanding your fertility signs is a helpful foundation for teaching the method.

Closing the Loop

Samuel and I met two more times before I left for the US and wrapped up our NGO recertification, a bundle of financial, administrative, and activity reports. We both felt elated afterward, having worked hard to meet the requirements and deadlines.

Chapter 24. We're On the Air!

So is my word that goes out from my mouth: It will not return to me empty, but will accomplish what I desire and achieve the purpose for which I sent it.

Isaiah 55:11 (NIV)

Evaluating New Programs for the PRC

It is October 2018. This time, I am planning to spend five weeks in Uganda. As always, I visited the PRC first and discussed our radio program, *Life Matters*. "Shall we have guests, how often, and how shall we facilitate them?" I stressed that we needed objectives for each program and no more than three points to get across. Repetition and examples are effective ways to share information. These programs are educational and present information from a Judeo-Christian worldview while providing guidance and encouragement to our listeners.

We discussed the Collier Community Abstinence Program (CCAP) and planned a trial in the schools and churches. At a *Humanae Vitae* conference in California, I met Renate, who introduced me to the CCAP. It was tested in Florida and found effective at decreasing teenaged pregnancies, our target population, and sexually transmitted diseases. Renate equipped us with manuals for teachers and students, letters of recommendation, online teachers' videos, and numerous studies documenting its effectiveness. I researched abstinence-based approaches and felt comfortable offering the CCAP, their preferred approach to youth sexuality education.

Budgeting for the St. Raphael Hospital

I am working on several budgets with Professor Vincent B. I take advantage of our meeting to inquire how best to occupy the land. The St. Raphael team evaluated several ways to utilize the hundred acres before beginning construction. We considered planting forests to act as natural boundaries and wind barriers and provide revenues from selling wood, or we could start farming portions of the land. Vincent suggested wire fencing in some areas, posts, and a few signs. He believes it is too early for farming. Without fencing, animals would wander and eat our crops. Eventually, the team decided to implement signs and posts and begin planting trees as soon as possible.

Health Insurance Is Picking Up!

Cyprian shared the progress we are making in spreading the concept of health insurance in the region. We have 1,500 insured members, and most of them are students. The health provider is earning profits and reinvesting them to improve health services, just as the plan suggested. I am ecstatic!

Cyprian proposes that we make it easier for groups of families to sign up by lowering the percentage requirement. At the moment, 60 percent of members of that group must agree to offer health insurance through their organization. If we lower it to 40 percent, the people that will sign up will be the ones that have sick family members. They are always the first to sign up. We must register healthy members as well to at least break even. HealthPartners are the ones that set the parameters. We are so fortunate that they remain involved in Uganda.

A Logo Is Born!

Cyprian announced the hospital needed a logo. I prayed about it and quickly drew a triangle to represent God, rays with nuggets of gold to portray the Holy Spirit, and the hospital's name spread out over the triangle sides. In the middle, I added: where God heals, both in English and Runyoro. It took five minutes. When I returned to California, I visited a professional logo designer. We inserted the triangle within a circle and added an open book and a banner to indicate a teaching institution. Knowing God is an advantage because He is ever-present and willing to help!

We're on the Air!

I joined Emily for the radio program. We will do part two on the harmful effects of divorce, especially on children. The information came from an article I wrote for *LifeWatch*, a publication of Alliance for Life International: "The Marriage Premium, a Huge Benefit."[14] Emily offered the same information in Luganda. Here is some feedback:

- From Paul, the guesthouse manager: "I loved it. I thought about calling during the show, but I did not want to miss the information being presented."

- From Geoffrey, staff at the guesthouse: "I loved the show; I learned so much. You now belong to Uganda. You're like an African mom to us."

- From one caller after we went off the air: "I liked the detailed information. I had not realized the negative impact of divorce on children."

- From another caller after the program: "I was planning to get a divorce. I am reconsidering."

There were some negative vibes. Our radio technician looked very sad afterward. We sought to address divorce from a children's perspective. What they suffer is serious. Couples assume that it will be best for their children in the long term. They do not realize that the harm lasts a lifetime.

Our Partners Are Coming Together

Vice Chancellor Dominic N., representing the Hoima bishop, called to say he was in Kampala and would like to meet with me before 4 p.m. Rhoda said it would take us three hours to get there in the afternoon traffic. Undisturbed, the vice chancellor said he would meet me in Muyenga and come by boda. I invited him for wine and appetizers at Hotel International since the chancellor was planning to have dinner during his last appointment. Chancellor Dominic is bright, articulate, animated, and cheerful, a young priest in his thirties, with a slew of responsibilities under which he thrives.

He recommended we form an ad hoc committee to direct the hospital project, including members from the Hoima diocese, the Bujuni parish, and ALI-UG. He welcomes a copy of the MOU at this stage and the implementation plan. Our partner wants to take a more active role in the hospital project, and I welcome it.

The next day, Rhoda and I drove to Nkozi to meet with Professor Michael M., an administrator at UMU. He welcomed the plan as above. Professor M. explained the different types of institutions we need to consider.

As I parted with Professor M., I extended a gift of cologne. It evoked a ready smile. I asked if he was married. He nodded and said, "My wife will love it too!" I added seven medical books, a donation from Mission Hospital in Mission Viejo, California. He was delighted.

Chapter 25. Every Encounter Matters

> But make sure that you don't get so absorbed and exhausted in taking care of all your day-to-day obligations that you lose track of the time and doze off, oblivious to God.
>
> Romans 13:11 (MSG)

Back in Uganda in April 2019, for one month, I settled quickly and visited the staff at the PRC. This time, I'm staying at Apricot Guesthouse for the first week since Christian Glory is full. Rhoda's mom owns Apricot. It is upscale for me, but Rhoda obtained a favorable rate for which I am very grateful. After distributing CCAP workbooks, children's clothing, USB drives, and the regular goodies, we discussed our goals for the next six months, including CCAP implementation and an employee handbook describing their benefits.

I followed up with teaching on maintaining a healthy lifestyle. I spent extra time with Emily, going over challenging aspects of her work as a Billings teacher. We rejoiced when she reported that a couple who had been trying to achieve pregnancy for five years got pregnant. I recall meeting with the client six months ago. She understood her fertility but was obsessing over it. I told her to stop charting and go with the flow. I am glad it worked.

Land Mines

I met an Italian reporter who was doing an investigation on land mines left over from the wars in the Gulu regions. The Uganda government said the area was mine-free since 2012, but accidental injuries from these war gadgets were still happening. This young man was paying for his expenses, hoping he would secure publication in a major magazine.

I told him his reporting would have a significant influence on his readers. Then I recounted how a *Time* magazine presentation on maternal mortality in Sierra Leone and Afghanistan[15] influenced me to start the Buwenge hospital project in Uganda. He was very encouraged. I prayed for wide diffusion and God's intervention in eliminating land mines once and for all.

Every Encounter Matters

While in Kibaale, I got to know Taddeo, the security person and groundkeeper at Sunset Guesthouse. He is married and has four children, ages five to thirteen. He visits them once a month for three days. On all occasions, including serving the public at the guesthouse, Taddeo wore torn-down clothing. I decided to go shopping with him and bless him with two or three new outfits.

While Taddeo was trying pants and shirts, I talked to Philip, the owner. I complimented him on his shop: best quality and selection in a clean and orderly environment. Shirts were tucked and wrapped in their see-through plastic covering, piled high on open shelves, and pants were neatly folded and displayed by style and color.

Philip found three pairs of pants and two shirts with a collar that met Taddeo's taste. I encouraged Philip to keep looking for another shirt as I teased him, "Never let a customer leave with less than she wants to spend. If I find it here, it saves me from going to Kampala, so work hard for me."

The young owner was gracious and engaging, so I kept sharing advice. I asked, "Do you know the success rule?" He did not but was willing to learn. I continued, "You get at least a high-school diploma, you get a full-time job, you get married, and then you have children."[16] I added, "And if your girlfriend gets pregnant, do not make it worse by having an abortion."

Philip welcomed it all and kept thanking me. He said he was a *born-again Christian*. I added, "Do not spend your profits on girls, gambling, or partying. Find a good Christian girl and get married." Philip was so thankful when I concluded by praying for him and his business.

As for Taddeo, I added a cologne and a leather belt. He was beaming with joy and confidence and anxious to go home to visit his family. I enjoyed the process more than he did since "it is more blessed to give than to receive" (Acts 20:35b, NIV).

The Ad Hoc Committee

During my stay, I took several steps to form an ad hoc committee as recommended by Chancellor Dominic. First, I was not sure who should form this committee. I soon realized that it would not come to pass unless I took the initiative. I prepared a plan, invited twelve people representing the existing St. Raphael committee, the HCD, and UMU, and appointed a time and place. I submitted my candidacy as a chairperson and invited others to do the same at the meeting if interested. I reached Godfrey. He informed me that the diocese was involved and would provide further guidance.

I was already back in Kampala when Godfrey and Cyprian came to visit. The fact that I am in Uganda for four to six weeks helps to speed up deliberations and, to some degree, decision-making. My team knows how important it is to show progress.

Godfrey reported that the Hoima diocese would appoint its committee. We parted on that note after concluding with prayer.

All the delays in advancing the St. Raphael Hospital project during this trip, including the funding needed to build the hospital, forced me to reevaluate my calling in initiating the project. Had I heard God correctly, or was I presuming on Him? As an exercise, I began to review all the steps, revelations, and progress we had made so far, most of them covered in these writings. I concluded that God had been consistent and present, guiding, blessing, and providing for His work. Donations always came timely and in just the right amount for the step at hand, the manna for the day.

True, there had been a slowdown. Would our partner join us at this stage or wait for more significant funding? As I was waiting, I was concerned about a sudden rise in kidnappings; there were three unrelated incidents over the last few days. Was the enemy trying to discourage me? I resolved to be cautious but remained in faith. The word for today was to believe that the Lord was working it out, "And these signs will accompany those who believe [...]" (Mark 16:17a, NIV). I was to renew my mind and remember that we serve a good God.

Chapter 26. Let's Give This One a Chance

The LORD will perfect that which concerns me; Your mercy, O LORD, endures forever; Do not forsake the works of Your hands.

Psalm 138:8 (NKJV)

Bank Matters

Back in Uganda in September 2019 for the next month, I visited Centenary Bank in Kampala, their flagship branch. The manager, Patrick, asked me how I would rate their services. I gave them an eight.

"Why not a ten?" he asked.

I said, "All is well when I'm here, but while in California, I lose track since I do not have access to my account online."

He set me up at once for internet banking. I have been happy ever since!

I usually go to traders to obtain the best exchange rate. I get out with large amounts of cash in Uganda shillings, then deposit it in the bank. It is dangerous for me and Rhoda to carry large sums in the car. I asked Patrick for negotiated rates at competitive prices. He obliged and instructed two tellers to give me access. Patrick requested something in writing about the work of the alliance in Uganda. I carried it out promptly. The banker is an asset to our organization.

Hospital Expansion Summit

Cyprian and I attended a two-day conference at the Sheraton Hotel in Kampala. It was a lovely affair, especially since we were invited. Most presentations were very technical. However, I managed to learn a lot. For example, loans for hospital equipment, design planning, and specialty care were impractical and almost impossible to secure.

We made great connections and intended to go and visit the pediatric facility CURE in Mbale and a new fistula specialty hospital in Soroti. We particularly enjoyed a presentation from a hospital administrator in Tanzania. He invited our team to visit. We looked into it but found it would be too expensive to travel to Tanzania as a team. As for the other two facilities, there were delays in securing an invitation. It would not be possible during my stay.

Advancing Our Work at the PRC

I met with the PRC staff, and we went over all our programs. We discussed each mother and how to meet their particular needs. Emily and I discussed our upcoming BOM teacher training. We are all involved in promoting the CCAP, our new abstinence-education program. We are seeking authorization to teach it in parish schools in Kampala. I shared how we obtained this program at great expense since I had to go to Florida to get it. I brought additional luggage containing workbooks for the last three trips to Uganda. We studied how to get it approved and met two experts to guide the process. Even so, no answer to our submission.

The staff suggested we move along and do our own thing. So far, we have never been able to teach our entire sexual integrity education program, the one we were using before the CCAP. Teachers would allow us an hour here and there, and never with the same group of students. We were not able to measure our impact. I am hoping it will be different with the CCAP.

The school must commit to the whole program for any number of kids they select. I am determined to pursue this goal. The next day, our manager called and told me I had a 9 a.m. appointment with Fr. Stephen at the diocese to discuss the CCAP. I prayed, "'Not by might nor by power, but by my Spirit,' says the LORD Almighty" (Zechariah 4:6, NIV).

I got acquainted by recalling that my son shared his name. Fr. Stephen was kind and friendly. He asked about the work of the alliance and what brought me to serve in Uganda. We discussed the CCAP, and Fr.

Stephen said that the church would be developing its own program. When he suggested we try with a smaller diocese, I received it as a confirmation that we should pursue our efforts to teach it in Kibaale. Fr. Stephen has been to Southern California and several states. He kept me for two hours as we discussed many subjects. When I shared the St. Raphael Hospital project, I mentioned we had big goals even though we were a small NGO. He quickly added, "That's because you're an American. Americans have big goals."

A Simple Dinner with Wine

Godfrey and Cyprian made it to Christian Glory House for a meeting. Since we were not going to Tanzania as planned, we needed time to wrap things up before I left. They arrived four hours later than planned because of the traffic. They were exhausted. I invited them to Caffe Roma for a late lunch and brought a bottle of sweet red wine. Godfrey had tears when I surprised him by asking if he wanted some. He added, "That would be very nice, Ms. Louise." Restaurant dining and wine are infrequent occasions in Uganda. Cyprian, forever a businessman, said he would investigate how to make wine. We left some for his wife, so he can convince her it's a good idea!

I brought up how the project funding would come together. I was basing this on my impressions after seeking God in prayer. They were all ears. The hospital—donations from Christian donors; the golf course—contributions from doctors who will come to Uganda and stay in the guesthouse; the guesthouse—from myself when I sell my home in California. From Godfrey echoed a resounding, "No! Ms. Louise, you can't sell your house in California!"

God is Taking Care of Mom

I arrived thirty minutes late at church on Sunday, as I did not remember the correct time. The church was packed, so the attendant added an extra chair. I was sitting behind a very old lady in the back. She kept dozing and almost fell off her chair. So I put my hand on her upper arm to steady her. I watched her as she walked and sat on the last bench at the end of the service. I slipped a bill in her hand and asked a nun nearby how the elderly lady would get to her home since she had no one with her. The sister knew her well and said she would leave early evening, using her cane. I prayed for her before I left as I gave her another bill. I still remember her toothless smile, shining eyes, and hands grabbing mine to say thank you.

She reminded me that my mom was getting more fragile and elderly. Our family had transferred her to assisted living but with extra care. When our mother went to the dining room, she noticed some patients needed help with feeding while others were not *with it*. When my sister Michelle visited her, she found our mother sad, quiet, and reflective. We hoped she would adapt quickly as my brother Jacques the doctor, reminded us that mom had been hospitalized six times over the last ten months and had fallen twice in the previous ten days.

When I was helping the elderly lady at church, I thought about my mom. I relaxed when I realized that God was taking care of her.

Will There Be a Next Time?

Cyprian and I needed to get back to Kibaale, but Cyprian had left his car there. We found Alex (fictitious name), who was anxious to make money by driving us in his small car. He was not a professional driver, but neither were we. It rained all the way to Kibaale. He did well until we reached Mubende and embarked on the new freeway, a two-way traffic road for the last seventy miles. In Uganda, we drive on the left side of the road. I asked him to use the defogger because we could hardly see anything. Often, cars coming toward us did not have their lights on. He was driving in the middle of the road, or sometimes, totally to the right without apparent reason. It scared me so much that I yelled. Alex kept doing it, as he was afraid to slip to the left even though it was a paved road. By the grace of God, we made it to Sunset! When he arrived back in Kampala, well before traffic time, he texted me that he would do better next time. I do not know if there will be a next time!

Everything Gets Done

Msgr. John Mary K. came to visit Sunset Guesthouse. He agreed to review the CCAP and pass it on to Fr. Andrew, the person in charge of such programs at the local secondary school. Godfrey is the founder/

director of St. John Secondary School. He said he is also interested in this program. He is my fallback guy for a pilot program.

Godfrey and I went to Centenary Bank in Kagadi to open the St. Raphael Hospital project bank accounts. We chose a branch closest to the project to make it easier for signatories. The staff assured me it would get done before I left.

Philip was working on the designs that weekend. He had questions; I had answers.

"Need elevator?"

"No, we use ramps."

In Uganda, elevators are useless most of the time because of breakage or electricity shortages. It will be a stand-alone building. Therefore, Philip said it would require additional space for the cafeteria, laundry, X-rays, pharmacy, etc.

"Should it grow in height or width?"

"We stay at three-story. Another wing for a utility building is better."

Philip noticed we had answers. It must be the Holy Spirit. Three years ago, everything was a big question mark.

Andrea (fictitious name) is my usual airtime provider. She has a little booth in town, open seven days a week. I encouraged her to train someone to cover for her on Sundays because everyone needs time off. Andrea said she would try. When I told Andrea that I noticed she hired someone, she said that she is trying to go to church on Sundays. Her relationship with her partner (or husband) is precarious.

I said, "Let's pray."

She said, "Oh, let's pray for a new one."

"Let's give this one a chance!"

Andrea smiled, and I said, "Find something he does well and compliment him. Tell him you need him to do that because he does it better than anyone else."

Some men do not think they are needed anymore and live without a purpose. She agreed and said she would try.

"I'll see you in six months," I said.

Walking to Sunset, I felt emotional as I looked around at the poverty and the muddy and slippery roads. Even so, I am getting attached to the area and the people. I pray for them often and for progress: better electricity, water, internet, and businesses. I pledged to learn Runyoro during my next stay. I want to communicate and merge better.

God Is on the Move

The St. Raphael leaders held a meeting with the architect in Kampala. We met at Jicca Hotel on the patio as we needed sufficient space to spread the drawings. Dark clouds were gathering, soon joined by thunder and lightning. We barely escaped for cover to a pavilion nearby, seeking to protect the drawings from the rain. We were preparing our submission to the Kibaale District for the pediatric facilities. Some team members needed computers or cell phones. I asked Anatoli to submit an estimate. Philip shared he had chest pain the night before, attributed to a persistent cough. I was more concerned about stress, and we prayed earnestly for Philip. The Holy Spirit's presence remained with us while traveling back to Kibaale. Everyone requested prayers.

Billings Ovulation Method Teacher Training in Kampala

It had been eight years since we held a training session in Kampala. I responded to a need expressed by Fr. Opio, president of Human Life International. He felt that leaders should have a breadth of understanding supporting pro-life and pro-family values. He brought several people with him: three lawyers, one psychologist, and many office staff. Emily recruited nurses, counselors, and teachers. We held it at Christian Glory House; they have beautiful conference facilities.

Fr. Opio taught the United Nations' perspective on sexual and reproductive rights and their involvement in Africa. We trained seventeen new teachers. The majority will exercise their new knowledge by learning about their fertility, and others will teach families and friends. The exception, like Emily, will make a career over it and will reap great rewards.

This training concluded my time in Uganda. It brings mixed feelings. Toward the end, I often get impatient with daily inconveniences, but it is harder to leave behind friends, staff, and evolving projects.

Chapter 27. The Covid Year

They will have no fear of bad news; their hearts are steadfast, trusting in the LORD.

Psalm 112:7 (NIV)

After attending a conference in West Africa in March 2020, it was my goal to spend the next six weeks in Uganda. The Covid pandemic changed my plans, and I stayed for nine months. In Benin, Emily and I attended a regional WOOMB International conference where twenty African countries sent representatives. Being fluent in French and English gave me a significant advantage. I could relate to participants from French-speaking African countries such as Benin, Congo, Cameroon, Senegal, Mali, and others. Emily shared her experience with teaching the Billings method to an illiterate population in Uganda.

I was encouraged by the level the method knowledge was spreading in Africa. It is taking off in all sectors: religious, medical communities, and laypeople. When God called me to teach it in Africa in 2005, He must have appointed others to do the same.

Meeting the Covid Wall

Arriving in Uganda at 2 a.m., I became the first beneficiary of COVID-19 restrictions implemented on March 13. After getting my temperature checked and filling out a health questionnaire, the attendant saw my US passport and said that people from the US were to quarantine first upon entering Uganda. I quickly pointed out that I had spent the last ten days in Benin, an African country that was not on the suspect list. She checked with her supervisor and allowed me to enter without conditions. I did not know much about Covid, having left the US when the pandemic was in its early stages. I knew enough to realize I had barely escaped fourteen-day isolation in a tent at the airport! I recalled with gratitude a promise the Lord had given me two years earlier, "The Lord will watch over your coming and going both now and forevermore" (Psalm 121:8, NIV).

I learned that there were 200–300 cases in the US and six deaths. In Orange County, where I live, there were seventeen cases, but only four a few days before. I did not like the arithmetic! I assumed that I would have to stay in Uganda until travel restrictions were lifted. Strangely, I was at peace; there were no cases in Uganda.

Rhoda and I got caught in a flooded street in town. She was apprehensive. Seemingly under the influence of anointing, I prayed fervently that the Lord would lift our car above the waters. The flooded area covered a long stretch, but we did fine.

Meeting in Kampala

The hospital project's leaders came to Kampala to meet with Philip and me. Everyone was amazed I had made it into the country under the Covid guidelines. It had taken four days to reconnect my phone and the internet because I arrived over the weekend. Therefore, no one knew I had made it. They thought I was in quarantine somewhere. We greatly rejoiced to see each other and be able to work on the project.

Philip has agreed to charge us only the bare minimum for his work. He was trying to find engineers who would do the same. We prayed that he would find a few good souls. Over the next five weeks, they will be working on construction drawings. The building committee under Chair R. E. vetted seven construction firms. After serious consideration, the project leaders chose Sarick Construction.

By March 21st, Covid had spread to 148 countries, but it had not come to Uganda. The next day, Uganda registered its first case, a Ugandan who had returned home from Dubai. The health department was doing contact tracing and infection-control measures they were familiar with, having used them with Ebola and other outbreaks.

We were to teach abstinence education for the first time in Kibaale, but the schools closed before our first class. I was back in Kibaale since there were less intense restrictions in rural areas. In Kampala, the military was policing the streets, people were shuttered in their homes, and our office was closed. The army resorted to caning offenders until President Museveni pleaded with the population to cooperate. He also asked law enforcement to use more appropriate methods to ensure compliance.

On March 26, the first opportunity to return to the US came about. Charter planes would be leaving Uganda for Europe and the US every ten to fifteen days while the airport was closed. It was expensive, $3,500 to $5,000 one way, but it allowed me to reevaluate my situation here and at home and determine where God wanted me. It gave me peace of mind, knowing that I could go back to the US if I needed to.

God Heard My Pleas

I resolved to work on developing the content of a dedicated website found at www.straphaelhospitalproject.org. The lack of reliable electricity and a computer battery that only lasted one hour frustrated my efforts. That morning, I started work in the guest lobby, my preferred office setting. The computer stopped, and there was no electricity. I returned all the materials to my room and vented my frustration to the Lord, "How can I do my work in these conditions? It is beyond me!" Then the fan in my room started working. I went back to the lobby and worked till 5 p.m. For the following three days, I marveled that I had electric power during the day.

Being in Uganda for longer than planned and under Covid restrictions brought problems. Accessing my bank accounts in the US and renewing my medications and visa were constant preoccupations. Still, the Lord resolved each situation. My son Steven helped numerous times while Cyprian did the same in Uganda.

We received gifts of fruits every time we ran out. Anatoli came with freshly picked pineapples, passion fruits, and avocados. By the middle of May, I had 2,300 Uganda shillings under my name (seventy-five cents). It needed to last me one week until I could travel back to Kampala. We were all in the same situation, living day to day under God's watchful eye and provisions.

Learning Runyoro

Anticipating that I would be in Uganda for several months, I resolved to learn Runyoro, the local language in Kibaale and Hoima District. Cyprian introduced me to his sister Florence, a retired school teacher, who agreed to give me lessons.

Having learned greetings, I practiced them with Raymond and Anita as we walked the grounds. Raymond tells me he is sad now that the schools are closed. He wants to become an optician, while Anita wants to be a doctor. I asked if they had prayer requests. Raymond asked for a useful mind. It is the same as asking for wisdom, which is unusual for a ten-year-old.

Their grandmother Mathilda came to visit often. We sat on the house ledge, and I practiced my Runyoro. She said that she loved me *muno, muno* ("a lot!"). These precious people are getting under my skin!

Shops were reopening, which led me to town, buying airtime while using Runyoro numbers, greeting the pharmacy and grocery store staff, and using my little Runyoro book to request what I needed. I divided it into sections, which made it easy to use. Everyone was excited to see my progress.

Work on the Land Begins!

On April 18, Godfrey called excitedly and shared that the district workers were clearing and grading our land where the pediatric facilities will be standing. Anatoli rushed to the site to gather pictures of the big yellow tractor and crane as evidence! We proudly displayed them on our website.

Philip from Envision Design Architects submitted a cost estimate for his supervision on the site once construction began. I told him our team was reviewing a construction contract that would include it. Philip exclaimed, "I'm supposed to supervise them [contractor's workers]; I should not get in bed with them!"

We laughed heartily.

Teaching the Billings Ovulation Method, Saving a Marriage

I was planning to return to Kampala in a few days. In the meantime, I prayed that God would open doors for me to teach the Billings method. A young man, Alex, returned to Sunset for the weekend. His wife and three boys, ages seven, five, and two, lived in Kampala. He was very curious, so I talked to him about the method. After learning the basics, he said, "Would you teach me?" So I did, and he grasped everything very quickly, including the teaching about using the method to conceive a girl. I noticed he drank too much. His drinking friend had a car accident over the weekend when he ran into a tree, totaled his car, and suffered a concussion. I prayed that this experience would influence Alex to return to his family and seek opportunities to work closer to home.

What a Difference a Day Makes!

Back in Kampala for one week, I visited with the staff at the PRC. We discussed all our programs and how to reach our clients during Covid. While Rhoda was driving at slow speed on Ggaba Road and with the windows down, I noticed a young girl on the side of the road, with her pleading eyes and her hand extended toward me for money. She appeared dirty, sweaty, weak, and even despondent. I quickly pulled a bill and gave it to her. I had never seen someone so desperate. We were driving by the area the next day, and I noticed the same girl. This time, she was smiling, even dancing when she saw me, still gesturing with her hands for a donation but not pleading. In a way, she was saying, "Please continue to care for me, see how better I am doing." Naturally, I obliged. I will never forget this little girl; every time she comes to mind, I pray for her.

Celebrating my Birthday

Back in Kibaale, the staff decided to celebrate my birthday. I invited the local project leaders and their wives, but it did not work out. Finally, those who came were guesthouse neighbors and the staff: neighbors John and Sylvia, Mathilda, and her grandchildren, Anita, Raymond, and Anthony; the house staff, Ruth, Joel, and Sylvia. Ruth prepared a delicious African dinner, including chicken appetizers, matoke, rice, beef stew, and cooked vegetables, displayed on nicely dressed tables outside. John dropped by with a birthday cake, a rare find.

We enjoyed western music, wine and beverages, gifts of sweets and field flowers from the children, and a water bottle from Ruth. Everyone was super excited to celebrate a birthday, a rare occasion in most households.

Joel, the young security guard at Sunset, was sitting next to me when he commented, "My life is starting today." When I asked why, Joel said, "I want this to be my life, celebrating occasions with my family and friends." It reminded me of King Solomon's wisdom,

> This is what I have observed to be good: that it is appropriate for a person to eat, to drink, and to find satisfaction in their toilsome labor under the sun during the few days of life God has given them—for this is their lot.
>
> Ecclesiastes 5:18 (NIV)

When Someone Prays for Favor

I was back in Kampala for one week to keep up with the PRC and ensure that Christian Glory had minimal operating revenues. I was still the only guest for the last four months. After Paul prepared a delicious Sunday dinner of rice, fish, vegetables, and pineapple, I joined him and the house staff for praise songs and prayers. I prayed for Christian Glory and its owner, Mary, to make it in these challenging times. Paul and the group prayed for favor as I carried out my work in Uganda.

The next day, I went to the bank to complete eight transactions at five different counters. I was expecting it would take at least two hours. I took a ticket for corporate banking and proceeded to a readily available teller. That was favor. She asked me how come I smiled often. I am not sure how she noted that since I must have been wearing a mask. I may have taken it down to speak to her through the window. I answered, "Because God is in my life."

The next teller was helping me with exchanging money from USD to Ugandan shillings. He told me the rate was not favorable. Even so, he exceeded my bottom line by twenty Ugandan shillings per dollar. That was favor. I was picking up a checkbook at another counter, and the teller asked me to sign in six different places. A young man next to me guided me on where to sign. That was favor. I finished all the transactions within sixty-five minutes, another blessing.

I was to meet Cyprian in the bank but could not guess when he would arrive in the lunch traffic. I sat down for two minutes until he surprised me with a greeting. I left the bank and found Rhoda had parked in front of the bank as allowed by the security guard. Usually, she had to find a parking space ten or fifteen minutes away. That was another favor.

Paul asked how my day had gone when I returned to the guesthouse. It was the perfect opportunity to praise God and thank Paul for praying for me.

We Are Winning the War!

We faced many obstacles in servicing our clients under Covid restrictions even though we reopened the office. Schools were closed; therefore, we couldn't reach students with abstinence education or sewing lessons for new mothers. Clients seeking to learn natural family planning or pregnancy counseling couldn't come to the office because transport costs had increased. Emily couldn't host our radio program because of curfew; therefore, the station had been playing reruns.

I perceived these widespread difficulties as an attack from our common spiritual enemy, and I went to war in prayer. I asked the staff to brainstorm and recommend other ways to service our clients. "Think outside the box" is our new motto!

We negotiated better terms and a new radio time slot and offered to reimburse transport fare. I returned to the office and noticed pregnancy counseling in progress while Emily taught a young lady how to use the Billings method to achieve pregnancy. We signed up two new teachers for the teacher-training correspondence course. We are preparing to teach the CCAP on the radio for the next five weeks. We rejoiced and gave praise to God for being back in business at all levels.

The Contract

The St. Raphael team visited a two-story office building that the chosen contractor had built eight years ago. It served as the Wakiso District headquarters in a Kampala suburb. We were doing due diligence before we contracted with the same construction company. We were pleased with the quality of the materials and artistry, the modern architecture, and the intact structure.

ALI-UG contracted to construct a three-story hospital and a one-story utility building. The church is not joining us at this time. We will proceed in phases and pay as we go, a concept that will allow us to fundraise locally and internationally as we continue building. We had already agreed on the price. It remained to go over all the clauses, determine the phases, down payment, terms, contingencies, etc. We decided to start with the foundation of the pediatric hospital, a goal that represented a good start. The team stayed overnight at Christian Glory House, and we rejoiced over reaching this milestone.

The Twenty-Four Questions

Soon after my return to Kibaale, Chancellor Dominic called. A team of experts had prepared a series of questions relating to governance issues, and he would like the St. Raphael committee to answer them. Once we reach an agreement, we will amend the MOU between ALI-UG and the HCD. The amended MOU will provide the foundation for a new company to guide the hospital project.

The committee went to work and submitted the answers within one month, along with land surveys, water investigations, architectural designs, district project approval, and other studies. We were excited because the diocese was preparing to come on board. Then we waited. We guessed by the questions and our answers that we were far apart. We met on the land to pray, and others joined us in spirit. We inquired, and Chancellor Dominic asked us to be patient as experts considered the way forward.

Godfrey and Anatoli determined that we were stuck and recommended we look at only three contentious clauses in the MOU. Msgr. John Mary K. came to the rescue. He represented the diocese, but he was also present since the project's inception. He clarified some issues. Professor Vincent B. served as a consultant for both the diocese and the alliance. Then the churches finally reopened. I will always believe that it had a profound impact on the diocese. How can you enter into a far-reaching agreement when you have been shuttered for months?

A Historic Event

Before my return to California, the HCD and ALI-UG held an event at the Bujuni parish. Bishop Vincent K. presided over the signing of our MOU and appointed members of an ad hoc committee. He commissioned them to form the company that would administer the hospital project.

There were forty-five guests in attendance, including government officials, church leaders, and friends of the project. We all moved to the site where Bishop K. dedicated and blessed the land. As members of this new committee, we felt a great sense of accomplishment over having the diocese join us and move forward together from this point on.

Chapter 28. A Future Missionary Meets an Old One

Even youths grow tired and weary, and young men stumble and fall; but those who hope in the LORD will renew their strength. They will soar on wings like eagles; they will run and not grow weary, they will walk and not be faint.

Isaiah 40:30–31 (NIV)

Thank God for Praying Friends

I returned to Uganda in March 2021. My desire to stay for six months required intense preparations. I did not take the time to write an email requesting prayers for my trip, but Muriel, Sergio, Debbie, Stephen, Dennis, and Brigitte texted they were praying as usual.

I soon discovered how vital their prayer coverage would be. I am sure Eithne prayed for memorable encounters because there were several during my flights. Unsettling happenstances resolved quickly. Here are only a few.

I was sitting next to Megan, a marketing executive. I began looking for my phone on the empty seat between us. I checked everywhere and concluded it had vanished. I heard myself say, "My heart is full of hope; it's probably in my carry-on."

My neighbor looked at me incredulously as she began her search. She found my phone in the space between us and gently noted that I could not see it because the phone cover was the same color as the seat and away from my field of vision. She had not responded to any of my comments denoting my faith. The Lord pointed out that this event was for her benefit.

At the restroom in the airport, my prescription glasses fell from the counter without a sound. When I turned to leave, I noticed that I had been a hair's breadth away from stomping on them.

On the next plane, I could not find my neck cushion. It probably fell from my carry-on at the previous airport. Since it was not the first but the third time this happened, I told the Lord that I was mad at myself and would not replace it.

During the flight, I sat next to Dennis, a Ugandan who had been visiting friends in the US. The work I do under the alliance and for his people touched him deeply. By then, I had caught on to the spiritual battle at play in all those unusual occurrences. I recalled a scripture that comforted me, "The righteous person may have many troubles, but the LORD delivers him from them all" (Psalm 34:19, NIV).

I was joking with God, telling Him that we were almost at our destination; how would He fix that?

We were standing and waiting to deplane in Amsterdam when Dennis asked if I had gotten some rest. I said, "Hardly any; because I lost my neck cushion."

He said, "Well, I just bought this one because people told me I needed one. You can have it; see, it's new."

I was ecstatic but trying to be cool. The Lord had done it again! I will not lose it this time because it has a secure attachment like my own with God.

A Future Missionary Meets an Old One

On the last flight, I sat next to twenty-year-old Sabrina from Seattle. She was planning to join a group of church friends in Uganda. They were setting up a little hospital and attending orientation. She would care for their children on-site during the next three weeks. It was her first mission trip. It was not smooth sailing (or flying!) for her either. Her Covid test was deemed too old to meet Amsterdam's requirements. She had to spend an extra night at the airport and repeat the test. Naturally, we compared stories.

She said that she usually finds out why a particularly distressing event is happening, so I asked her, "Why this one?"

She answered to my amazement, "God delayed my first flight so that I could meet you."

A future missionary met an old one.

A Word of Prophecy

Soon after my arrival, Cyprian called and gave me this word of prophecy, a first for him: "You are God's messenger to Kibaale and the Hoima diocese. One of the purposes of the hospital is very important. It is to practice Hippocratic medicine and protect conscience rights." Cyprian said that God revealed to him that this project is much bigger than the team, for it is God's project, and He will find donors to finance it. I received the promise and hid it in my heart.

I have several goals to accomplish during the next six months: start a bakery, form a new company, appoint a board of directors to direct the hospital project, begin to write this book, practice my Runyoro, complete a project proposal, supervise the PRC, and seek opportunities to evangelize. Let's see what God is up to.

Starting a Bakery

I visited with the PRC staff and discussed opening a bakery and school under our NGO, a process I initiated in 2020. I looked for rent in Kabalagala, a business center in Kampala, but I found the prices very high. Robinah, our landlord at the PRC, visited. Her son Ivan was building a duplex in Gayaza; she asked if I would be interested in relocating there.

The staff knew the location and were all excited about it. It offered a mix of residential and business properties in a growing area. We took a field trip to the region and fell in love with it. Ivan was building two identical units side by side. For the moment, both businesses could occupy one side. When we started the bakery school, we could each have our own. The price was affordable, five times cheaper than in Kabalagala.

Below our PRC in Munyonyo, there was a bakery. I interviewed baker Jovan and learned much from him. I hired his teacher Philip as a consultant, and we visited the competition in Kampala and Gayaza. Philip and I chose our bakery equipment and bought pots, pans, and supplies. Ivan, his wife, and I selected tiles, flooring, and paint colors; it turned out beautiful.

Our bakery equipment vendor is engineer Ronald. He teased me that we were building a California bakery. He worked with Henry, our electrical expert, to customize the outlets. Electricity was an issue from the start. We needed high-grade electricity to accommodate our powerful bakery equipment. Since the area was under construction, the electrical infrastructure was not present, and it became our responsibility under the watchful eye of Henry and the local utility company.

We have finally secured three-phase electricity and are planning to open the bakery in September 2022. Uganda is growing by leaps and bounds, and electric power has not kept up with the increasing demand; a dam is under construction.

Saving a Marriage

I was returning to Christian Glory House when I got into a conversation with a woman reclining on a blanket in the front yard. I learned that she was from Congo and spoke only French. So, we connected well since I had been in Congo. Cecilia (a fictitious name) was there to visit with her husband, Pierre (fictitious name). He worked for Doctors without Borders as a manager. They had two sons, ages thirteen and four. I noted the age difference, and she quickly explained in French, "My husband is never there; he can be gone one to nine months at a time." When she couldn't take it anymore, she would come for a visit. She was sad and reflective.

I felt a strong desire to encourage her. I told her that I understood how she felt because when I was in my twenties, my husband traveled half the time, and I was very lonely. I affirmed her for being here and doing all she could to maintain the bond between her and Pierre, the father of their two children. I inquired if she had a solid social network at home.

"Do you speak on the phone with Pierre at least every other night? What about the children? They also need a strong connection with their dad."

She told me it was tough and acted like she was at the end of her rope.

I went on, "Cecilia, this is your life; accept it. If it were not for this problem, it would be another. Life is demanding without him, but wandering is not an option. Cecilia, do you go to church with the children?"

She hugged me, crying on my shoulders, and thanked me for telling her these things. They may have been on the brink of separation because she was so thankful for my intervention. Two days later, they were both leaving for Congo. Pierre had requested two weeks' vacation to be with the children. I keep in touch with Cecilia when she comes to Uganda to visit her husband.

What's in a Name?

The ad hoc committee met regularly to discuss the articles of association and the constitution. Robert and Florence, both lawyers, guided the process. As project initiators, Louise and Chancellor Dominic took a particular interest in its development with expert guidance from committee members. We used our MOU as a foundation and worked hard to achieve a meaningful document that would inspire us for years to come.

On a rainy Sunday afternoon, Chancellor Dominic and I discussed the company registration. Then, we talked about what led to the revised MOU, the famous twenty-four questions. I said, "This could have led to a divorce before we ever got married!"

The Chancellor quipped, "The last five years were our courtship."

The partners formed a company, St. Raphael Healing and Wellness Center Ltd. It will direct the hospital project and other health-related ventures. We rejoiced because its name carries our objectives: to operate a mission hospital focused on healing and disease prevention and with Jehovah-Rapha, our healer.

Moving Forward Together

I returned to Uganda in January 2022. During my three-month stay, the partners completed the registration process for the new company and appointed board members and committees. The board studied and assumed the existing construction contract. I plan to return in July to oversee the opening of the bakery and witness the first foundation stone being laid, God's promise to me when the hospital project started. It is found in Zechariah:

> [...] This is the word of the LORD to Zerubbabel: Not by might, and not by power, but by my spirit, says the Lord of hosts. Who are you, O great mountain? Before Zerubbabel you become a plain. He will bring forth the first stone amid shouts of "Favor, favor be upon it!" Then the word of the Lord came to me: The hands of Zerubbabel have laid the foundations of this house, and his hands will finish it. Thus you shall know that the Lord of hosts has sent me to you. For whoever has scorned such a day of small things will rejoice to see the capstone in the hand of Zerubbabel.
>
> Zechariah 4:6–10 (NABRE)

Closing Comments

I hope this book helps alleviate your fears about going to the mission field. Fear is a normal response to the unknown, but as a child of God, we can be assured of His presence no matter where we serve Him. Be aware that the enemy of your soul will always try to stop you from stepping out in faith to follow your calling. Again, he will attack no matter what you plan to do as a child of the King. Christ will deliver you from his grip and bring you to a place of freedom, for Jesus said, "So if the Son sets you free, you will be free indeed" (John 8:36, NIV).

You may expect a certain level of trepidation; even so, fear should not stop you from stepping into your destiny. Joyce Meyer, a renowned teacher and evangelist, said, "Do it afraid"[17] in her latest book.

Do you want to live the abundant life that Jesus promised His followers? You will find it in serving Him, hidden like a gem in a grass pile. When you least expect it, the joy of serving Him bubbles up in your soul, and you can hardly contain your amazement at what He has planned for you out of your act of surrender.

As you are a child of God, He calls you to do more. He wants you to use the talents he has generously bestowed on you. He desires you to share your time and skills with the less fortunate so that your generosity will supply their needs.

Is God concerned about the poor? His Word says, "'For the oppression of the poor, for the sighing of the needy, now I will arise,' says the Lord. 'I will set him in the safety for which he yearns'" (Psalm 16:6, NKJV).

Are you wealthy? Then you have a greater responsibility. Serve Him with it. Consider the cause of the poor who do not have their basic needs met and suffer daily from ill health.

We hope to have inspired you to join us on one of our trips to Uganda (www.allianceforlifeinternational.org). You will be free to explore how you can give back and live a passionate life of service to God and those less fortunate.

We will always have the poor with us. I believe that God wants it this way because it allows us to find Christ, serve Him, and take our inheritance:

> Then the King will say to those on his right, "Come, you who are blessed by My father; take your inheritance, the kingdom prepared for you since the creation of the world." […] The King will reply, "Truly I tell you, whatever you did for one of the least of these brothers and sisters of mine, you did for me."
>
> Matthew 25:34, 40 (NIV)

Discover the abundant life with us, the one that God prepared for you from the foundation of the world.

About the Author

Originally from Quebec, Canada, Louise moved to Southern California in 1978. She is an RN by profession. Louise holds a bachelor of science in nursing from California State Dominguez Hills and a master of arts in international human rights from Simon Greenleaf University in Anaheim, California, now known as Trinity Law School in Santa Ana, California. She is also a certified teacher and teachers' trainer of the Billings Ovulation Method.

Louise retired as an RN case manager for a large health-maintenance organization in California. She has held several administrative positions during her long career, including pediatric head nurse and director of nursing in a home-health agency. She is a writer, speaker, and teacher.

In 2001, Louise was privileged to meet with the secretary of the Pontifical Academy for Life in Rome and present him with a Model declaration of the human rights of the preborn child, the subject of her master's thesis.

Since 2003, Louise has taught the Billings Ovulation Method to healthcare professionals and parish and village people in Congo, Uganda, and Kenya. She has trained over 450 new teachers from all over Uganda.

Since March 2010, Louise has attended the Commission on the Status of Women sessions, a yearly United Nations conference held in New York. She represents the World Organization of the Billings Ovulation Method (WOOMB International).

In 1998, Louise founded Alliance for Life International (ALI), a Christian, nonprofit human-rights organization based in California. ALI's mission is to affirm, defend, and live out the built-in and equal value and dignity of all members of the human family, from their earliest phase of development to their natural end.

ALI's concern for human life also extends to those who reside in socially disadvantaged countries where the lack of essential medical care reflects severe health disparities and often results in shortened lifespans. It leads ALI to cooperate with leaders to improve medical care. The St. Raphael Teaching Hospital project of Western Uganda represents ALI's commitment.

Endnotes

1   Maathai Wangari, *The Challenge for Africa* (New York City, NY: Penguin Random House, 2009).

2   Rachel Weisshaar, "The Challenge for Africa: a Conversation with Wangari Maathai," New Security Beat, May 5, 2009, www.newsecuritybeat.org/2009/05/the-challenge-for-africa-a-conversation-with-wangari-maathai.

3   Weisshaar, "The Challenge for Africa: a Conversation with Wangari Maathai."

4   WHO-Uganda 2013.

5   Wikipedia, s.v. "Healthcare in Uganda,"last edited May 26, 2022, www.en.wikipedia.org/wiki/Healthcare_in_Uganda.

6   Wikipedia, s.v. "Healthcare in Uganda."

7   WHO-Uganda 2013.

8   Jiaquan Xu, Sherry L. Murphy, Kenneth D. Kochanek, and Elizabeth Arias, "Mortality in the United States, 2015" Centers of Disease Control and Prevention, December 2016, www.cdc.gov/nchs/products/databriefs/db267.htm.

9   Kibaale District, Uganda, Bureau of Statistics, 2009; maternal deaths in the US, CDC, 2012.

10   Kibaale District, Uganda, Bureau of Statistics, 2009; child mortality in the US, CDC, 2014.

11   WHO-Uganda 2013.

12   CIA World Factbook 2014.

13   "How many women and girls die in childbirth?" Maternity Worldwide, accessed July 29, 2022, www.maternityworld-wide.org/the-issues.

14   1. Louise Allard, "The Marriage Premium, a Huge Benefit," *LifeWatch*, a publication of Alliance for Life International, June 2016, www.allianceforlifeint.org/publications/life-watch-newsletters-other.

15   "Dying to Give Birth: One Woman's Tale of Maternal Mortality," Time Inc., accessed July 29, 2022, www.content.time.com/time/video/player/0,32068,89844377001_1994479,00.html.

Lynsey Addario, reporter and videographer relate the story of an eighteen-year-old mother, Sessay, who gave birth to twins in Sierra Leone. Long labor; difficult delivery. Doctor showed up when she was already dead. In Sierra Leone, women have one in eight chance of dying in childbirth; in the US, it is one in 4,800. Sierra Leone and Afghanistan are the worst countries on the earth for dying in birth.

16   W. Bradford Wilcox, Wendy Wang, Alysse ElHage, "*Life*

Without Father: Less College, Less Work, and More Prison for Young Men Growing up Without their Biological Father," Institute for Family Studies, accessed July 29, 2022, www.ifstudies.org/blog/life-without-father-less-college-less-work-and-more-prison-for-young-men-growing-up-without-their-biological-father.

17   Joyce Meyer, *Do It Afraid* (New York City, NY: FaithWords, Hachette Book Group, 2020).

CPSIA information can be obtained
at www.ICGtesting.com
Printed in the USA
BVHW042027150223
658591BV00013B/473

9 798887 381299